Quick SHORT RECIPE COOKBOOK

The Confident Cooking Promise of Success

Welcome to the world of Confident Cooking,
where recipes are double-tested by our team
of home economists to achieve a high standard
of success—and delicious results every time.

bay books

C O N T E

Creamy Potato and Silverbeet Soup, page 17

Traditional Garlic Prawns, page 42

Potato Gnocchi with Tomato Olive Sauce, page 23

Steak with Mushroom and Wine Sauce, page 61

The test kitchen, where our recipes are double-tested by our team of home economists to achieve a high standard of success and delicious results every time.

Apple Puff Squares, page 105

Citrus Delicious, page 101

Front cover photograph, clockwise from top left: Eggplant Sandwiches, page 93; Chicken with Lemon and Basil Sauce, page 68; Prawn and Tomato Salad with Ginger Dressing, page 47.

Inside front cover photograph: Swiss Onion Tart, page 81.

Back Cover: Corn and Capsicum Fritters, page 90.

When we test our recipes, we rate them for ease of preparation. The following cookery ratings are on the recipes in this book, making them easy to use and understand.

A single Cooking with Confidence symbol indicates a recipe that is simple and generally quick to make —perfect for beginners.

Two symbols indicate the need for just a little more care and a little more time.

Three symbols indicate special dishes that need more investment in time, care and patience—but the results are worth it.

The Publisher thanks Waterford Wedgewood for their assistance in the photography for this book.

Tandoori Chicken Skewers, page 73

Caesar Salad, page 84

Quick Short Recipes

These recipes were especially compiled with today's busy cooks in mind.
They feature short lists of ingredients readily available at any supermarket and they can
be prepared quickly. One thing they're not short on, however, is flavour.

Family meals are a test of organizational skill. First you need to decide what to prepare, then the pantry has to be checked for ingredients, then any necessary shopping must be done. Finally, there's the preparation and serving of the food.

You won't have to make an expedition to specialist food stores to put together any of the recipes in this book. Once you've stocked your pantry with the basics, you should only need to supplement them with fresh, locally available produce.

We've made suggestions here for the pantry contents, but your own pantry will reflect the tastes and preferences of you and your family.

These recipes are designed to have you spend a minimum of time in the kitchen. Although some take a while to cook, they can all be prepared quickly. Do this when you get home and relax during the cooking time.

Minimising preparation time does not mean compromising on nutritional value, quality of ingredients or the final product. It just means being organized so that you'll have more of that precious leisure time.

Remember that fresh ingredients when available are always preferable to dried, canned or frozen foods. Use your discretion when shopping. Buy fresh ingredients in season rather than canned ones.

In most cases, fresh ingredients do not take much longer to prepare. If, on the other hand, you want to try a recipe that includes vegetables such as spinach or peas that are out of season, substitute frozen or canned varieties. Don't buy wilted or stale vegetables—choose a substitute.

Some convenience items, such as bottled pasta sauces, ready-made stocks and frozen pastries, can also be used to save time.

STOCKING THE PANTRY

Follow these suggestions and you will always have the beginnings of a nutritious meal on hand.

Staples needed include flours, sugar, salt, pepper, rice and pasta, potatoes and onions. As well, stock your pantry with a range of spices, condiments and canned goods. Make sure you have good supplies of your favourite, much-used ingredients.

Replace pantry stock when it runs out or, in the case of canned goods that keep for a long time, stock up on your favourite brands when you see them 'on special'.

As well as the condiments listed, for quick curry-making you'll need things such as Thai sweet chilli sauce, ready-made curry pastes, and sambal oelek (a mixture of chopped chilli and salt). Some condiments need to be refrigerated after opening—just follow the instructions on the bottles.

Other necessities include refrigerated items such as margarine, butter, milk, eggs and cheeses.

PURCHASE & STORAGE

Onions

All members of the onion family are invaluable in the kitchen—always have a selection on hand. Choose firm onions with dry, papery skins; avoid sprouting specimens or any that feel spongy. Onions should be stored in a cool, dry, dark place, or refrigerated.

Brown onions have a stronger flavour than white, will store well and are excellent for making casseroles and soups. White onions are milder in flavour and do not store as well. Use them raw in salads.

Red onions can also be used raw in salads. Store them in the refrigerator.

To spare your eyes, place onions in the freezer for 15 minutes, or refrigerate for about an hour, before peeling.

INGREDIENTS FOR THE PANTRY

➤ Basics	➤ Dried herbs	➤ Stock
flour	basil	beef
olive oil	bay leaves	chicken
onions	mixed herbs	vegetable
pasta	oregano	(Stock is available in
pepper	rosemary	powder form, cubes
potatoes	thyme	or tetra packs.)
puréed tomato		
rice	➤ Spices	➤ Cans
salt	cardamom	chickpeas
sugar	cinnamon	coconut milk
tomato paste (purée)	cloves	corn niblets
vinegar	coriander	creamed corn
	cumin	fruit
➤ Condiments	curry powder	kidney beans
soy sauce	garam masala	salmon
tabasco	ginger	three-bean mix
tomato pasta sauce	nutmeg	tomatoes
Worcestershire sauce	turmeric	tuna

A well-stocked, organized pantry will make planning easier for cooks with many other demands
on their time. Check the contents often and make sure frequently used items are replaced.

Potatoes

The humble potato or 'spud' is probably the most versatile of all vegetables. There are many varieties sold commercially. Desiree and pontiac are two of the most common and popular.

Often potatoes are not identified and are simply sold as 'old' or 'new'. The difference is in their age, not in the type or variety.

'New' potatoes are any variety which has been dug before reaching maturity. They are usually smaller and sweeter than 'old' potatoes. They contain less starch than floury potatoes and are therefore best for chips, salads and roasts.

Potatoes come brushed, washed or unwashed. If they are brushed or washed, check they haven't been bruised in the process. Sometimes it is better to buy them unwashed.

The most important distinction between potatoes to bear in mind is whether the variety is 'waxy' or 'floury'. If you're not sure which type to use for a particular purpose, ask your greengrocer.

Waxy: Most 'new' potatoes, as well as most red varieties, are waxy. They contain less starch than floury potatoes. Waxy potatoes won't fall apart when boiled and are therefore best for salads. Use them for roasts and chips as well. Don't use them for mashing.

Floury: Most 'old' potatoes, on the other hand, are floury and have a higher starch content, having converted their sugar to starch. This makes them excellent for baking in their skins, or mashing, as they have a fluffier texture. If you're using them for salads or chips, soak the peeled potatoes in water before cooking.

'Old' potatoes must be stored in a cool, dark, dry place. Light will cause them to go green. It is better to buy potatoes loose, not pre-packaged. If they are only available in plastic packaging, remove the plastic before storing. Throw away any potatoes that have turned green.

'New' potatoes do not keep as well as 'old' potatoes, so buy them in small quantities as required and refrigerate in a paper bag. The skin is relatively thin—don't peel, just rub any blemishes off the skin.

Don't store potatoes near onions as the potatoes will tend to rot.

Garlic

Garlic should be bought when firm. Make sure the cloves are not withering in their skins. Garlic will keep at room temperature for several weeks.

Garlic adds a delicious flavour to casseroles, soups, marinades, sauces, stir-fries and vegetable dishes. Add whole, peeled cloves to salad dressing for a subtle flavour. Garlic is easy to peel if you press down on the clove with a flat-bladed knife or cleaver.

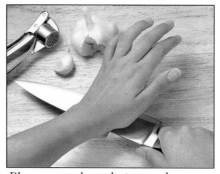

Place on a board, press down on clove with flat-bladed knife or cleaver.

The skin will come away readily, making it easy to remove.

Ginger

Ginger, like garlic, should be plump when bought, not dry and withered. Keep it in a cool, well-ventilated place, or wrap in foil and refrigerate. It will freeze successfully.

When peeled and either finely chopped or grated, ginger can be used to add flavour to stir-fries, marinades, curries and vegetable dishes. A little can be included when making your own fruit juice.

Tomatoes

The versatile tomato is processed and sold in many ways. We have a choice of chutneys, canned tomatoes, tomato paste (purée), tomato sauce, special pasta sauces and sundried tomatoes.

Whole tinned tomatoes can be chopped with kitchen scissors.

Tomatoes, raw or cooked, are used in combination with garlic, herbs and cheeses to make anything from simple salads, to casseroles and bolognaise sauce and spicy curries.

Fresh tomatoes are available throughout the year. Choose firm fruit of a suitable colour, type and size for your needs. If you want to use them straight away, choose rich red. For use later, choose pink to light red tomatoes. Green tomatoes can be bought for ripening at home as long as you have a cool place for them. Don't buy blemished, bruised or split tomatoes.

Store tomatoes in the pantry or on the kitchen bench, not in direct sunlight. If they get too hot while ripening, the flavour doesn't develop as well. It is too cold in the refrigerator for tomatoes. In the heat of summer you can refrigerate ripe tomatoes for a few days but the flavour will deteriorate. The ideal ripening temperature for tomatoes is about 20°C.

REFRIGERATOR ITEMS

Cheeses

There is an enormous variety of cheeses available at the supermarket—check the 'use-by' date when buying. Cheddar and Parmesan are used in many recipes.

Buy Parmesan cheese in block form from your delicatessen and store wrapped in foil in the refrigerator. If mould forms on the edges, cut the mould off before use.

Wrap cheese in foil or kitchen paper; avoid using plastic wrap. Refrigerate in the dairy compartment, on a shelf on the refrigerator door, or near the bottom section of refrigerator. Refrigerate soft cheeses such as cottage cheese in a covered container.

Eggs

Eggs are best kept in the refrigerator. To prevent them freezing, do not store them near the back of the refrigerator where it is colder, or near an ice compartment.

Vegetables and Fruit

Vegetables and fruit are best bought as close as possible to the time you're going to use them. However, as it is not always practical to shop daily, they can be bought weekly as long as you're careful how you store them.

Generally, most will keep in the refrigerator for about a week. Don't buy fruit and vegetables that are bruised or discoloured. Green vegetables and salad ingredients should not be dried out or yellowing.

Buy vegetables such as carrots, beans, broccoli, asparagus, celery and fennel when they are firm and crisp. They are best stored in plastic bags in the crisper section of your refrigerator. Trim celery and store the same way. Special lettuce containers keep lettuce crisp. If you don't have one, remove the core by cutting it out or twisting it and store whole lettuce or leaves in a plastic bag in the crisper. Trim some of the dark green tops off spring onions (scallions) and wrap in a damp tea towel before refrigerating. Capsicum (peppers) and cucumber can be placed straight in the crisper. If you don't have a crisper, use plastic containers, freezer bags or plastic bags for storage in your refrigerator. Wipe mushrooms clean and store them in paper bags in the crisper; they will keep for a few days. Avocados should be refrigerated when ripe.

Most fruits are best kept in the crisper in the refrigerator once they are ripe, although bananas and lemons prefer room temperature. Berries should be spread out as much as possible for storage.

Herbs

Always keep a selection of dried herbs to liven up your cooking. Use our suggestions or your favourites.

An amazing assortment of fresh herbs is now available from greengrocers. Substitute fresh for dried if you wish: dried herbs have a stronger flavour so use at least three times as much fresh herb as you would dried.

Fresh herbs don't keep very long so buy when you need them. Store them in your crisper in plastic bags or wrapped in a damp tea towel. Wash and dry before use.

Herbs such as chives, parsley, mint and basil can be grown easily in the garden or in pots. Freshly picked herbs are convenient and delicious.

A FEW TIPS

DRIED BEANS can be prepared in two ways. The quickest way is to place them in a pot, cover with water to about 5 cm (2 inches) above beans. Bring to boil over high heat. Boil for 2 minutes, cover and remove from heat. Allow to stand for 1 hour. (Some, such as chickpeas, may need a little longer.) Drain, cook for at least 1 hour or until tender. If you have more time, cover beans in the same way with water and soak for at least 4 hours or overnight. If you cook too many beans you can freeze the excess for future use.

Canned beans can be substituted to eliminate soaking and cooking time. Drain and rinse before use.

Boil beans for 2 minutes. Remove from heat, cover and leave 1 hour.

STIR-FRYING is a quick, efficient method of cookery developed in Asia.

Prepare all ingredients before starting. This doesn't take long and once you have done it cooking time is fast. Vary the ingredients for a different flavour and texture each time.

Cut meat and chicken into uniform-sized pieces. Slicing meat is easier if you freeze it first and slice with a very sharp knife while still quite firm.

Cut vegetables such as carrots, celery and zucchini (courgette) into julienne strips of equal size and broccoli into small florets. Onions and leeks should be very thinly sliced.

TO MAKE BREADCRUMBS from stale, leftover bread for use in stuffings, remove crusts and cut up or break the bread into pieces and place in a food processor. Process until crumbs are desired size. Place in freezer bags, seal and freeze for future use. If you want to crumb food, process bread in the same way and then place on an oven tray, in a 180°C (350°F/Gas 4) oven, until brown, before freezing.

Break or cut bread into pieces and place in food processor.

Process until breadcrumbs are the size you need.

FREEZE IN ICE-CUBE TRAYS for future use things such as lemon juice, tomato paste (purée), passion-fruit pulp or leftover wine. When frozen, remove from ice-cube trays and keep in the freezer in sealed bags.

Tomato paste (purée) and similar leftovers can be frozen for future use.

Speedy SOUPS

LEEK AND POTATO SOUP

Preparation time: 15 minutes
Total cooking time: 25–30 minutes
Serves 4

3 rashers bacon
1 tablespoon oil
2 large leeks, sliced
500 g (1 lb 2 oz) potatoes,
    peeled and chopped
1 litre (4 cups) chicken
    stock

➤ CHOP BACON, discard rind.
1 Heat oil in a medium pan. Add
bacon and stir over medium heat for
3 minutes or until lightly golden.
Drain on paper towels.
2 Add leek to pan. Stir over medium
heat for 5–10 minutes until soft. Add
potato and stock, bring to the boil.
Reduce heat to low; cover. Simmer,
stirring occasionally, for 20 minutes or
until potato is tender.
3 Remove pan from heat; allow mixture to cool slightly. Transfer mixture,
in batches, to food processor or
blender and process until smooth.
4 Return mixture to pan and add
bacon, salt and pepper. Heat through
and serve. Garnish with a sprig of
fresh herbs, if desired.

COOK'S FILE

Storage time: This recipe can be
made up to 3 days before required.
Store, covered, in refrigerator.
Hint: Discard dark green tops of the
leeks as they are tough. Use only the
white and pale green parts. Wash
leeks thoroughly before use to remove
dirt and grit.

9

PUMPKIN AND CUMIN SOUP

Preparation time: 10 minutes
Total cooking time: 15 minutes
Serves 4

1 kg (2 lb 4 oz) pumpkin
500 ml (2 cups) chicken stock
1 onion, chopped
2 cloves garlic, crushed
2 teaspoons ground cumin
80 ml ($^1/_3$ cup) coconut milk
1 tablespoon lemon juice

➤ PEEL PUMPKIN and chop into small chunks.

1 Combine pumpkin in a large pan with 250 ml (1 cup) water, stock, onion, garlic and cumin. Bring to the boil, reduce heat to low and simmer, covered, for 15 minutes or until pumpkin is tender.

2 Transfer mixture, in batches, to food processor or blender and process each batch until smooth. Return mixture to pan. Add coconut milk and lemon juice to pan, stir over medium heat until heated through. Garnish with chopped chives, if desired.

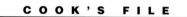

COOK'S FILE

Hint: Pumpkin can be cut into chunks, brushed with oil and baked in the oven until soft. Scoop the flesh from skin and process with simmered ingredients as above.
Variation: Thick (double/heavy) cream can be used instead of coconut milk. If you prefer a thinner consistency, use an extra 250 ml (1 cup) of stock.

SPLIT PEA AND HAM SOUP

Preparation time: 10 minutes
Total cooking time: 1–1¹/₂ hours
Serves 4–6

250 g (9 oz) green split peas
1.5 litres (6 cups) chicken stock
   or water
250 g (9 oz) ham off the bone,
   finely chopped
1 onion, chopped
2 cloves garlic, crushed
¹/₂–1 teaspoon dried mixed herbs
20 g (¹/₃ cup) chopped parsley

➤ PLACE SPLIT PEAS in large pan.
1 Add stock, ham, onion, garlic, herbs and parsley to pan; bring to the boil. Reduce heat to low and simmer, stirring occasionally, for 1–1¹/₂ hours or until split peas are soft and pulpy. Garnish with a sprig of flat-leaf (Italian) parsley, if desired.

COOK'S FILE

Storage time: Soup can be made up to 3 days before required. Store, covered, in refrigerator.
Hint: Off-cuts of ham are ideal for this recipe. Alternatively, you can use 2–4 rashers thick bacon. Remove the rind and chop roughly.

FRENCH ONION SOUP

Preparation time: 5 minutes
Total cooking time: 15–20 minutes
Serves 4

4 large onions
60 g (2¼ oz) butter
1 litre (4 cups) beef stock
8 slices baguette
125 g (½ cup) grated Cheddar
  cheese

➤ SLICE ONIONS thinly.
1 Melt butter in large pan, add onion. Stir constantly over medium heat for 5–10 minutes or until dark golden, being careful not to burn onion.
2 Add 250 ml (1 cup) water, bring to the boil. Reduce heat to low; simmer, covered, for 15 minutes or until onion is very tender. Add stock; bring to the boil. Simmer for 3–5 minutes.
3 Grill (broil) baguette slices on both sides. Top with grated cheese and grill (broil) for another minute or until

cheese has melted. Place toast in serving bowls and spoon soup over the top. Serve immediately.

COOK'S FILE

Storage time: Soup can be made up to 3 days in advance. Store, covered, in refrigerator. Grill (broil) bread slices just before serving.
Variation: Grilled (broiled) cheese on toast may be served separately if preferred. Grated Gruyère cheese can be used instead of Cheddar.

CORN CHOWDER

Preparation time: 5 minutes
Total cooking time: 25 minutes
Serves 4

1 onion
2 rashers bacon
30 g (1 oz) butter
750 g (1 lb 10 oz) potatoes,
    peeled and cut into
    small cubes
500 ml (2 cups) chicken stock
440 g (1 lb) can creamed corn
375 ml (1 1/2 cups) milk

➤ CHOP ONION and bacon.
1 Melt butter in large pan, add onion and bacon. Stir over medium heat for 3–5 minutes or until lightly golden. Add potato and stock; bring to the boil. Reduce heat to low and simmer, covered, for 10 minutes.
2 Stir in creamed corn and milk. Simmer, uncovered, stirring occasionally to prevent sticking, for 10 minutes or until potato is tender and chowder has thickened.

COOK'S FILE

Storage time: This recipe can be made up to 3 days before required. Store, covered, in refrigerator.
Hints: Do not allow soup to boil after milk has been added as it may curdle.
   For a heartier soup, add 350 g (12 oz) shredded barbecued chicken.

LENTIL AND VEGETABLE SOUP

Preparation time: 10 minutes
Total cooking time: 20 minutes
Serves 4–6

8 spring onions (scallions)
2 tablespoons oil
3 teaspoons curry powder
1.25 litres (5 cups) vegetable
   stock
250 g (1 cup) red lentils
425 g (15 oz) can tomatoes
250 g (9 oz) broccoli, chopped

2 zucchini (courgettes),
   sliced

➤ TRIM ENDS from spring onions.
1 Chop spring onions. Heat oil in medium pan; add spring onion. Add curry powder; stir over medium heat 5 minutes.
2 Add stock, lentils and undrained, crushed tomato; bring to the boil. Reduce heat to low, simmer, covered, 15 minutes or until lentils are tender. Stir occasionally to prevent sticking.
3 Add the broccoli and zucchini; simmer for another 5 minutes or until vegetables are tender.

COOK'S FILE

Storage time: This recipe can be made up to 3 days before required. Store, covered, in refrigerator. Soup may thicken on cooling as the lentils absorb the stock. If necessary, add a little water or vegetable stock to soup when reheating.
Hint: Serve with slices of fresh crusty French bread.
Variations: Brown, green, or yellow lentils are also suitable for this recipe. Cooking times may vary.

   Substitute other vegetables such as carrots or beans if you prefer. Vary cooking times accordingly.

LAMB AND PASTA SOUP

Preparation time: 10 minutes
Total cooking time: 40 minutes
Serves 6–8

2 onions
2 tablespoons oil
500 g (1 lb 2 oz) lean lamb
   meat, cut into 2 cm
   (³/4 inch) cubes
2 carrots, chopped
4 sticks celery, chopped
425 g (15 oz) can tomatoes
2 litres (8 cups) beef stock
270 g (3 cups) spiral pasta
chopped parsley, for serving

➤ CHOP ONIONS finely.
1 Heat oil in a large pan and cook cubed lamb in batches until golden brown. Remove each batch as it is done and drain on paper towels. Add onion to pan and cook for 2 minutes or until softened. Return meat to pan.
2 Add chopped carrot and celery, undrained, crushed tomato, and beef stock. Stir to combine and bring to the boil. Reduce heat to low and simmer, covered, for 15 minutes.
3 Add spiral pasta to pan. Stir briefly to prevent pasta sticking to pan. Simmer, uncovered, for another 15 minutes or until lamb and pasta are tender. Sprinkle with chopped parsley before serving.

COOK'S FILE

Storage time: This recipe can be made up to 3 days before required. Store, covered, in refrigerator.
Hints: Pasta can be cooked separately if you wish. Drain thoroughly and add to the soup before serving.

   Meat should be cooked quickly in batches to prevent it becoming tough.
Variations: For a lighter flavour, use half stock and half water. Vegetable stock may be used instead of beef.

   Add chopped fresh or dried herbs towards the end of cooking time. Rosemary, mint, parsley or thyme would all be suitable.

   Other types of pasta such as macaroni or shell pasta can be substituted.

Lentil and Vegetable Soup (top) and
Lamb and Pasta Soup

MUSHROOM SOUP

Preparation time: 10 minutes
Total cooking time: 25 minutes
Serves 4

2 onions
60 g (2¼ oz) butter
2 cloves garlic, crushed
500 g (1 lb 2 oz) small or
    medium mushrooms,
    chopped
30 g (¼ cup) plain (all-purpose)
    flour
560 ml (2¼ cups) milk
375 ml (1½ cups) beef stock
20 g (⅓ cup) chopped parsley
sour cream, for serving

➤ CHOP ONIONS finely.

1 Melt butter in a large pan; add onion and garlic. Stir over medium heat for 3 minutes or until onion is soft. Add chopped mushrooms to pan; stir 5 minutes. Add flour, stir for another minute.

2 Add milk and stock to pan; stir until combined. Bring to the boil; reduce heat to low. Simmer, uncovered, for 15 minutes or until mixture has reduced and thickened and mushrooms are tender. Stir in parsley. Serve with a dollop of sour cream.

COOK'S FILE

Storage time: This recipe can be made up to 3 days before required. Store, covered, in refrigerator.

CREAMY POTATO AND SILVERBEET SOUP

Preparation time: 10 minutes
Total cooking time: 10 minutes
Serves 4

1.25 litres (5 cups) chicken stock
750 g (1 lb 10 oz) potatoes,
    peeled and chopped
500 g (1 lb 2 oz) silverbeet
    (Swiss chard)
185 g (³/₄ cup) sour cream

35 g (¹/₃ cup) grated Parmesan
cheese

➤ PLACE CHICKEN STOCK and potato in a large pan and bring stock to the boil. Cover pan; reduce heat to low and simmer mixture for 5 minutes or until potato is almost tender.

1 Wash silverbeet thoroughly; drain. Using a sharp knife, remove stalks from silverbeet. Shred leaves and add to pan. Simmer, covered, for 3 minutes or until potato and silverbeet are tender. Add sour cream and Parmesan cheese and stir thoroughly to combine. Remove pan from heat.

2 Transfer mixture to food processor or blender in small batches. Process each batch until smooth. Return mixture to pan, stir over medium heat for 1 minute or until heated through. Garnish with chive flowers or other fresh herbs, if desired.

COOK'S FILE

Storage time: This soup can be made up to 2 days before required. Store, covered, in refrigerator.

Fast PASTA DISHES

SPINACH AND RICOTTA SHELLS

Preparation time: 15 minutes
Total cooking time: 15 minutes
Serves 4

20 giant pasta shells (conchiglie)
1 tablespoon oil
2 rashers bacon, finely chopped
1 onion, finely chopped
500 g (1 lb 2 oz) English
   spinach, chopped
750 g (1 lb 10 oz) ricotta cheese
35 g (¹/₃ cup) freshly grated
   Parmesan cheese
250 g (1 cup) tomato pasta
   sauce
toasted pine nuts, optional, for
   serving

➤ ADD PASTA shells to a large pan of rapidly boiling water and cook until just tender; drain.

1 Heat oil in pan; add bacon and onion. Stir over medium heat for 3 minutes or until lightly browned. Add spinach, stir over low heat until wilted. Add ricotta cheese and stir until combined.
2 Spoon mixture into pasta shells, sprinkle with Parmesan cheese. Place shells on cold, lightly oiled griller (broiler) tray. Cook under medium–high heat for 3 minutes or until lightly browned and heated through.
3 Place tomato pasta sauce in small pan, stir over high heat for 1 minute or until heated through. Spoon sauce onto serving plates, top with shells. Sprinkle with pine nuts, if desired.

COOK'S FILE

Storage time: Shells can be assembled with filling several hours before required. Store, covered, in refrigerator. Grill (broil) just before serving.
Variation: Use silverbeet (Swiss chard) instead of English spinach.

TORTELLINI WITH EGGPLANT SAUCE

Preparation time: 10 minutes
Total cooking time: 20 minutes
Serves 4

500 g (1 lb 2 oz) fresh tortellini
60 ml (¹/4 cup) oil
2 cloves garlic, crushed
1 red capsicum (pepper), chopped
500 g (1 lb 2 oz) eggplant
   (aubergine), chopped
425 g (15 oz) can tomatoes
250 ml (1 cup) vegetable stock
30 g (¹/2 cup) chopped basil

➤ ADD TORTELLINI to a large pan of rapidly boiling water and cook until just tender.

1 Drain pasta. Heat oil in a large pan; add garlic and capsicum. Stir over medium heat for 1 minute.

2 Add eggplant cubes and stir over medium heat for 5 minutes or until lightly browned. Add to pan the undrained, crushed tomato and vegetable stock. Stir to combine and bring to the boil. Reduce heat to low and cover pan; cook for 10 minutes or until vegetables are tender. Add basil and drained pasta and stir until well combined. Serve.

COOK'S FILE

Storage time: Sauce can be made a day ahead. Store, covered, in refrigerator. Cook pasta and reheat sauce just before serving.
Hints: Cut the eggplant just before using as it turns brown when exposed to the air.

Vegetable stock is available in cubes or tetra packs from supermarkets.

1

2

SALMON AND PASTA MORNAY

Preparation time: 10 minutes
Total cooking time: 10–15 minutes
Serves 4

400 g (14 oz) small shell
   pasta
30 g (1 oz) butter
6 spring onions (scallions),
   chopped
2 cloves garlic, crushed
1 tablespoon plain
   (all-purpose) flour
250 ml (1 cup) milk
250 g (1 cup) sour cream
1 tablespoon lemon
   juice
425 g (15 oz) can salmon,
   drained, flaked
30 g (1/2 cup) chopped
   parsley

➤ ADD PASTA to a large pan of rapidly boiling water and cook until just tender; drain.

1 While pasta is cooking, melt butter in medium pan; add onion and garlic. Stir over low heat for 3 minutes or until tender. Add flour and stir for 1 minute. Combine milk, cream and lemon juice in a jug. Add gradually to onion mixture, stirring constantly. Stir over medium heat for 3 minutes or until mixture boils and thickens.

2 Add salmon and parsley to pan; stir for 1 minute or until heated through. Turn hotplate off. Add drained pasta to pan, stir until well combined. Season with salt and pepper before serving.

COOK'S FILE

Storage time: Sauce can be made a day ahead. Store, covered, in refrigerator. Cook pasta and reheat sauce just before serving.

TAGLIATELLE WITH MUSHROOMS

Preparation time: 10 minutes
Total cooking time: 10–15 minutes
Serves 4

375 g (13 oz) tagliatelle
1 tablespoon oil
400 g (14 oz) button mushrooms
4 rashers bacon, chopped
1 onion, chopped
310 ml (1¼ cups) thick
    (double/heavy) cream
freshly grated Parmesan cheese

➤ ADD PASTA to a large pan of rapidly boiling water and cook until just tender; drain.

1 While pasta is cooking, slice mush-

1

rooms. Heat oil in pan; add bacon and onion. Stir over medium heat for 4 minutes or until brown. Add mushrooms and stir for another 2 minutes or until tender. Add cream and stir for 1 minute or until simmering. Remove pan from heat. Add tagliatelle to sauce, stir until combined. Serve with freshly grated Parmesan cheese.

COOK'S FILE

Storage time: Sauce can be made several hours ahead. Store, covered, in refrigerator. Reheat just before serving.
Variation: Chopped pancetta can be used instead of bacon, if preferred.

POTATO GNOCCHI WITH TOMATO-OLIVE SAUCE

Preparation time: 10 minutes
Total cooking time: 15 minutes
Serves 4

500 g (1 lb 2 oz) potato gnocchi
2 tablespoons oil
1 leek, sliced
250 g (1 cup) tomato pasta sauce
170 ml ($2/3$ cup) vegetable stock
50 g ($1/3$ cup) chopped black
    olives
6 anchovies, chopped

➤ ADD GNOCCHI to a large pan of rapidly boiling water and cook until just tender; drain.

1 While gnocchi is cooking, heat oil

in a large pan, add leek. Stir over medium heat for 2 minutes or until tender. Add tomato sauce, stock, olives and anchovies. Stir mixture over medium heat for 5 minutes or until heated through. Serve sauce poured over gnocchi.

COOK'S FILE

Storage time: Sauce can be cooked a day ahead. Store, covered, in refrigerator. Reheat just before serving.
Note: Potato gnocchi is available fresh from supermarkets and delicatessens. Use any other dried or fresh pasta, if preferred.

BUTTERFLY PASTA WITH PEAS, PROSCIUTTO AND MUSHROOMS

Preparation time: 10 minutes
Total cooking time: 10–15 minutes
Serves 4

375 g (13 oz) butterfly (farfalle)
  pasta
60 g (2¼ oz) butter
200 g (7 oz) mushrooms, thinly
  sliced

1 onion, chopped
250 g (9 oz) cooked peas
3 slices prosciutto, sliced
250 ml (1 cup) cream
1 egg yolk

➤ ADD PASTA to a large pan of rapidly boiling water and cook until just tender; drain and return to pan.

1 Heat butter in pan; add mushrooms and onion; stir over medium heat for 5 minutes or until tender.

2 Add peas and prosciutto to pan. Combine cream and yolk in a small

jug and add to pan. Cover; simmer for 5 minutes or until heated through.

3 Mix sauce through pasta or serve sauce over top of pasta. Top with shaved or grated Parmesan cheese, if desired.

COOK'S FILE

Hint: Reserve ¼ cup liquid when peas are cooked. Use to thin the sauce if necessary.

Variation: Add crushed garlic when cooking onion. Sprinkle with freshly chopped mint and parsley.

SPAGHETTI BOLOGNAISE

Preparation time: 10 minutes
Total cooking time: 1 hour 45 minutes
Serves 4

2 tablespoons oil
1 onion, chopped
2 cloves garlic, crushed
500 g (1 lb 2 oz) minced
   (ground) beef
425 g (15 oz) can tomatoes,
   chopped
4 tablespoons tomato paste
   (purée)
1 teaspoon dried oregano
1 teaspoon dried basil
375 g (13 oz) spaghetti
grated Parmesan cheese, for
   serving

➤ HEAT OIL in a large pan; add onion and garlic. Stir over medium heat for 2 minutes or until tender.
1 Add beef, cook over high heat for 3 minutes until well browned and almost all liquid has evaporated. Use a fork to break up any lumps of beef.
2 Add undrained, crushed tomato, tomato paste, oregano and basil; bring to the boil. Reduce heat to low, simmer, uncovered, stirring occasionally, for 1 hour 30 minutes or until sauce has thickened. About 20 minutes before end of cooking time, add spaghetti to a large pan of rapidly boiling water and cook until just tender; drain. Serve spaghetti in individual bowls with bolognaise sauce spooned over the top. Sprinkle with freshly grated Parmesan cheese.

COOK'S FILE

Storage time: Sauce can be cooked up to 2 days before required. Store, covered, in refrigerator. Reheat just before serving.

PENNE WITH SUNDRIED TOMATOES AND LEMON

Preparation time: 10 minutes
Total cooking time: 12–15 minutes
Serves 4

250 g (9 oz) penne
60 ml ($^1/_4$ cup) olive oil
3 rashers bacon, chopped
1 onion, chopped
80 ml ($^1/_3$ cup) lemon juice
1 tablespoon thyme leaves
50 g ($^1/_3$ cup) chopped sundried
    tomatoes
80 g ($^1/_2$ cup) pine nuts, toasted

➤ ADD PASTA to a large pan of rapidly boiling water and cook until just tender; drain.

1 Heat oil in a large pan. Add bacon and onion; stir over medium heat for 4 minutes or until bacon is brown and onion has softened. Add pasta to pan with lemon juice, thyme, tomato and pine nuts. Stir over low heat for 2 minutes or until heated through.

COOK'S FILE

Note: Sundried tomatoes will become bitter if heated too much.
Variation: Use pancetta instead of bacon, if preferred.

PESTO WITH TAGLIATELLE

Preparation time: 10 minutes
Total cooking time: 10 minutes
Serves 4

250 g (9 oz) spinach
   tagliatelle
100 g (2 cups) tightly packed
   basil leaves
4 cloves garlic, peeled and
   chopped
50 g ($^1/_3$ cup) pine nuts
100 g (1 cup) freshly grated
   Parmesan cheese
185 ml ($^3/_4$ cup) olive oil

▶ ADD TAGLIATELLE to a large pan of rapidly boiling water and cook until tender. Drain well; return to pan.

1 While pasta is cooking, place basil, garlic and pine nuts in food processor and process until finely ground. Add cheese; process until well combined.
2 With motor running, slowly pour olive oil through the feed tube. Add enough sauce to pasta to coat well. Season with salt and pepper before serving. Garnish with fresh basil leaves, if desired.

Storage time: Cook pasta just before serving. Pesto may be made in advance and kept in refrigerator. Spoon into a jar and cover sauce with a thin layer of oil.

Variations: Add extra 40 g ($^1/_4$ cup) toasted pine nuts just before serving.

Add 60 g (1 cup) fresh parsley and increase oil to 250 ml (1 cup).

SPIRAL PASTA WITH BROCCOLI AND HAM

Preparation time: 10 minutes
Total cooking time: 10–15 minutes
Serves 4

400 g (14 oz) spiral pasta
250 g (9 oz) broccoli florets
30 g (1 oz) butter
250 g (9 oz) leg ham, cut into strips
2 cloves garlic, crushed
6 spring onions (scallions), chopped
200 g (7 oz) mushrooms, sliced
250 ml (1 cup) thick (double/heavy) cream
30 g (½ cup) roughly chopped parsley

➤ ADD PASTA to a large pan of rapidly boiling water and cook until just tender; drain.

1 Cook broccoli florets in a small pan of rapidly boiling water for 2 minutes or until tender; drain. Heat butter in a large pan. Add ham strips and stir over medium heat for 2 minutes or until ham is lightly browned.

2 Add crushed garlic, spring onion and mushrooms, stir for 2 minutes. Add drained pasta, broccoli, cream and parsley; stir for 1 minute or until heated through.

COOK'S FILE

Storage time: This recipe is best cooked just before serving.
Hint: For best flavour, use leg ham off the bone.

MACARONI WITH CHEESE SAUCE

Preparation time: 15 minutes
Total cooking time: 30 minutes
Serves 4

200 g (7 oz) macaroni
60 g (2¼ oz) butter
1 onion, chopped
2 rashers bacon, chopped
30 g (¼ cup) plain (all-purpose) flour
625 ml (2½ cups) milk
½ teaspoon nutmeg
185 g (1½ cups) grated Cheddar cheese

➤ PREHEAT OVEN to 180°C (350°F/Gas 4). Add macaroni to a large pan of rapidly boiling water and cook until tender; drain.

1 Heat butter in a large pan; add onion and bacon. Stir over medium heat for 4 minutes or until tender. Add flour; stir over low heat for 1 minute. Add milk gradually; stir until mixture is smooth. Stir constantly over medium heat for 4 minutes or until mixture boils and thickens. Simmer over low heat for another minute. Remove pan from heat. Stir in nutmeg.

2 Stir in pasta and 125 g (1 cup) of the cheese. Spoon into greased 1.5-litre (6 cup) ovenproof dish. Sprinkle with rest of cheese and bake for 20 minutes.

COOK'S FILE

Note: Milk can be flavoured before use. Place in a small pan with a slice of onion, 6 peppercorns and a bay leaf. Bring to the boil. Remove from heat, cover and leave for 15 minutes; strain.

SPAGHETTI WITH FRESH TOMATO SAUCE

Preparation time: 15 minutes
  + refrigeration
Total cooking time: 10–15 minutes
Serves 4

4 spring onions (scallions)
4 firm ripe tomatoes
8 stuffed green olives
2 tablespoons capers
2 cloves garlic, crushed
$1/2$ teaspoon dried oregano
20 g ($1/3$ cup) parsley, chopped
80 ml ($1/3$ cup) olive oil
375 g (13 oz) thin spaghetti

➤ CHOP SPRING ONIONS finely.
1 Chop tomatoes into small pieces. Chop olives and capers. Place all ingredients, except pasta, in a bowl; mix well. Cover and refrigerate for at least 2 hours. Add pasta to a large pan of rapidly boiling water and cook until tender. Drain and return to pan.
2 Add cold sauce to hot pasta and mix well.

COOK'S FILE

Variation: Add 30 g ($1/2$ cup) of shredded fresh basil leaves.

1

2

RAVIOLI WITH HERBS

Preparation time: 15 minutes
Total cooking time: 4 minutes
Serves 4–6

2 tablespoons olive oil
1 clove garlic, halved
800 g (1 lb 12 oz) ravioli
60 g (2¹/₄ oz) butter, chopped
2 tablespoons chopped
    parsley
20 g (¹/₃ cup) chopped basil
2 tablespoons chopped chives

➤ COMBINE OIL and garlic in a small bowl, set aside.

1 Add ravioli to a large pan of rapidly boiling water and cook until tender. Drain well and return to pan. Add oil to pasta; discard garlic. Add butter and herbs to ravioli, toss well.

COOK'S FILE

Variation: Use fresh coriander (cilantro) instead of parsley.

1

POPULAR *Pasta* IN MINUTES

SALMON TAGLIATELLE

Cook 400 g (14 oz) tagliatelle in large pan of boiling water until tender; drain. Heat 60 ml (^{1}/4 cup) oil in pan; add 2 sliced onions, 3 chopped spring onions (scallions) and 2 sticks sliced celery. Stir over medium heat 3 minutes or until tender. Add 415 g (14 oz) can drained, flaked red salmon and 250 ml (1 cup) pomarola sauce; stir over heat 1 minute or until heated through. Add tagliatelle; stir. Season, to taste. Serves 4.

SALMON TAGLIATELLE

FETTUCCINE CARBONARA

Cook 500 g (1 lb 2 oz) fettuccine in large pan of boiling water until just tender; drain. Place 6 rashers chopped bacon in pan, stir over medium heat 5 minutes or until crisp. Add 610 ml (1^1/4 cups) thick (double/heavy) cream; heat until simmering. Pour into large bowl; add 50 g (^{1}/2 cup) grated Parmesan cheese and 4 lightly beaten egg yolks. Whisk quickly until combined. Add hot fettuccine; stir well. Garnish with chives. Serves 4.

FETTUCCINE CARBONARA

SPAGHETTI WITH LENTIL SAUCE

Cook 400 g (14 oz) spaghetti in large pan of boiling water until just tender; drain. Combine 250 g (1 cup) red lentils in pan with 750 ml (3 cups) vegetable stock, 2 chopped onions, 2 crushed garlic cloves and 1 teaspoon dried mixed herbs; bring to the boil. Reduce heat to low, cover pan; simmer 15 minutes or until lentils are tender, stirring occasionally. Add 125 ml (^{1}/2 cup) pomarola sauce, stir over heat until combined; do not boil. Add spaghetti, stir well. Serve with yoghurt. Sprinkle with chopped herbs. Serves 4.

SPAGHETTI WITH LENTIL SAUCE

PENNE WITH SALAMI AND TOMATO SAUCE

Cook 400 g (14 oz) penne in large pan of boiling water until tender; drain. Heat 1 tablespoon oil in pan; add 200 g (7 oz) sliced salami, cut into strips, and 1 onion, cut in thin wedges. Stir over medium heat 2 minutes. Add 250 ml (1 cup) puréed tomato, 170 ml (^{2}/3 cup) chicken stock and 1 tablespoon sugar; bring to boil. Reduce heat to low, simmer, uncovered, 2 minutes or until sauce has reduced and thickened. Add pasta and 2 tablespoons sliced basil, stir until combined. Serves 4.

PENNE WITH SALAMI AND TOMATO SAUCE

TUNA AND LEMON SHELLS

ZUCCHINI AND BASIL MACARONI

SPIRAL PASTA WITH MUSHROOMS AND PESTO

LINGUINE WITH SMOKED SALMON AND CAVIAR

TUNA AND LEMON SHELLS

Cook 400 g (14 oz) pasta shells in large pan of boiling water until tender; drain. Place in medium pan a 440 g (1 lb) can tuna, drained and flaked, with 80 ml ($^{1}/3$ cup) lemon juice, 80 ml ($^{1}/3$ cup) olive oil, 2 tablespoons chopped capers and 1 teaspoon chilli sauce. Stir over medium heat for 1 minute or until heated through. Add pasta, stir over heat until combined. Add salt and pepper, to taste. Sprinkle with freshly grated Parmesan cheese. Serves 4.

ZUCCHINI AND BASIL MACARONI

Cook 400 g (14 oz) macaroni in large pan of boiling water until tender; drain. Melt 60 g ($2^{1}/4$ oz) butter in pan; add 4 sliced zucchini (courgettes). Stir over medium heat for 3 minutes or until lightly browned. Add 1 tablespoon plain (all-purpose) flour and stir over low heat for 1 minute. Add 500 ml (2 cups) milk gradually, stirring until sauce is smooth. Stir constantly over medium heat for 2 minutes or until mixture boils and thickens. Add 155 g (1 cup) fresh or frozen peas and 20 g ($^{1}/3$ cup) chopped basil, stir over heat for 1 minute. Add macaroni, stir until combined. Add pepper, to taste. Sprinkle with Parmesan cheese. Serves 4.

SPIRAL PASTA WITH MUSHROOMS AND PESTO

Cook 400 g (14 oz) spiral pasta in large pan of boiling water until tender; drain. Heat 2 tablespoons oil in pan; add 400 g (14 oz) sliced button mushrooms. Stir over medium heat 3 minutes or until lightly browned. Add 500 ml (2 cups) vegetable stock and 90 g ($^{1}/3$ cup) pesto, bring to the boil. Reduce heat to medium, cook until mixture has reduced by half. Add pasta, stir until combined. Serve with a dollop of sour cream. Serves 4.

LINGUINE WITH SMOKED SALMON AND CAVIAR

Cook 500 g (1 lb 2 oz) linguine in a large pan of boiling water until tender; drain. Heat 1 tablespoon oil in a medium pan and add 1 sliced leek. Stir over low heat for 3 minutes or until tender. Add 310 g ($1^{1}/4$ cups) sour cream, 170 ml ($^{2}/3$ cup) water and 250 g (9 oz) sliced smoked salmon, cut into strips. Stir over medium heat for 1 minute or until heated through. Add 2 tablespoons chopped dill and 1 tablespoon red caviar, stir until combined. Spoon hot linguine onto serving plates, top with sauce. Serves 4.

Super SEAFOOD IDEAS

CRUMBED CALAMARI WITH CHILLI PLUM SAUCE

Preparation time: 25 minutes
Total cooking time: 12 minutes
Serves 4

500 g (1 lb 2 oz) calamari tubes
30 g ($^{1}/_{4}$ cup) plain (all-purpose) flour
1–2 eggs, lightly beaten
240 g (3 cups) fresh breadcrumbs
oil, for frying

Chilli Plum Sauce
1 teaspoon oil
1 clove garlic, crushed
315 g (1 cup) dark plum jam
80 ml ($^{1}/_{3}$ cup) white vinegar
1–2 tablespoons bottled chopped chilli or sweet chilli sauce

➤ RINSE CALAMARI tubes and pat dry with paper towels.

1 Remove spine and skin if necessary. Cut into 1 cm ($^{1}/_{2}$ inch) rings. Set aside.
2 Combine flour, salt and pepper in a plastic bag. Add calamari and toss to coat. Dip each ring into beaten egg, drain off excess; toss in breadcrumbs. Pat crumbs lightly onto rings, shake off excess. Heat 2 cm ($^{3}/_{4}$ inch) of oil in a frying pan until hot.
3 Fry a few calamari rings at a time, until golden. Drain on paper towels. Keep warm. Use slotted spoon to remove crumbs from surface of oil between batches. Serve rings hot, with a bowl of Chilli Plum Sauce. If desired, serve with wedges of lemon.
To make Chilli Plum Sauce: Heat oil in a small pan. Add garlic and cook until just starting to colour. Add jam, vinegar and chilli. Stir over medium heat until well blended. Thin with a little warm water if necessary.

COOK'S FILE

Hint: Serve with grilled fish fillets and mixed salad.

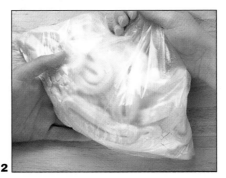

GLAZED GRILLED FISH

Preparation time: 10 minutes
    + marinating
Total cooking time: 8 minutes
Serves 4

2 tablespoons olive oil
2 tablespoons lemon juice
2 tablespoons fruit chutney
1 tablespoon honey
1 tablespoon chopped coriander
    (cilantro)
2 cloves garlic, crushed
4 snapper fillets

➤ COMBINE OIL, lemon juice, fruit chutney, honey, coriander and crushed garlic in a small jug. Place fish fillets in a large non-metal dish.

1 Pour oil mixture over fish. Cover and refrigerate for 1 hour.

2 Transfer fish fillets to cold, lightly oiled griller (broiler) tray and cook under high heat, brushing with remaining marinade occasionally, for 4 minutes each side or until tender. Serve with lemon slices, if desired.

COOK'S FILE

Storage time: Coriander mixture can be made several hours ahead. Brush over fish and cook just before serving.
Variation: Substitute any firm-fleshed fish such as salmon or ling.

TUNA AND VEGETABLE BAKE

Preparation time: 15 minutes
Total cooking time: 35 minutes
Serves 4

2 tablespoons oil
1 onion, chopped
1 red capsicum (pepper), chopped
2 zucchini (courgettes), chopped
425 g (15 oz) can tomatoes
425 g (15 oz) can tuna, drained
   and flaked
2 potatoes, coarsely grated
125 g (1 cup) grated Cheddar
   cheese

➤ PREHEAT OVEN to 210°C (415°F/ Gas 6–7).
1 Heat oil in pan; add onion, capsicum and zucchini. Stir over high heat for 3 minutes or until tender.
2 Add undrained, crushed tomato, reduce heat to low, simmer 3 minutes. Stir in drained, flaked tuna. Spread over base of a 1.5-litre (6 cup) ovenproof dish. Squeeze liquid from potato. Combine potato and cheese, spread over tuna mixture. Bake 25 minutes. Cook under hot griller (broiler) until crisp and golden brown.

COOK'S FILE

Hint: Use pontiac or old potatoes for this recipe.

FISH WITH MARJORAM AND LIME

Preparation time: 15 minutes
Total cooking time: 4 minutes
Serves 4

100 g (1 cup) dried
  breadcrumbs
2 teaspoons dried marjoram
1 teaspoon cayenne pepper
4 ling fillets
1 egg, lightly beaten
60 ml ($^1/_4$ cup) oil
2 tablespoons lime juice

➤ COMBINE breadcrumbs, marjoram and cayenne pepper on a sheet of greaseproof paper.
1 Brush fish fillets with egg, coat with breadcrumb mixture. Heat oil in pan; add fish. Cook over medium heat for 2 minutes each side or until tender and golden brown. Serve drizzled with lime juice. Garnish with fresh marjoram, if desired.

COOK'S FILE

Storage time: Fish can be coated in breadcrumb mixture several hours ahead. Store, covered, in refrigerator. Cook just before serving.
Variation: Any white, firm-fleshed fish fillets are suitable for this recipe.

CRUNCHY FISH FILLETS

Preparation time: 10 minutes
Total cooking time: 6 minutes
Serves 4

150 g (1/2 cup) cornmeal
4 bream fillets
60 ml (1/4 cup) oil
170 g (2/3 cup) mayonnaise
2 tablespoons chopped chives
1 tablespoon sweet chilli
   sauce

► PLACE CORNMEAL on a sheet of greaseproof paper or plate.

1 Cut diagonal slashes in skin of fish fillets. Press fillets in cornmeal to coat thoroughly. Heat oil in pan; add the coated fish.
2 Cook over medium heat for 3 minutes on each side, or until tender. Drain on paper towels. Combine mayonnaise, chives and chilli sauce. Serve with fish. Garnish with chervil, if desired.

COOK'S FILE

Storage time: Mayonnaise mixture can be made a day ahead. Store, covered, in refrigerator.
Hint: Serve with salad.
Variation: Any firm-fleshed fish is suitable for this recipe.

1

2

BEER-BATTERED FISH WITH POTATO WEDGES

Preparation time: 15 minutes
Total cooking time: 10 minutes
Serves 4

3 medium pontiac potatoes
oil, for deep-frying
125 g (1 cup) self-raising flour
1 egg, beaten
185 ml (³/₄ cup) beer
4 medium white fish fillets
plain (all-purpose) flour, for
    dusting
spice salt, to taste
125 g (¹/₂ cup) tartare sauce

➤ WASH POTATOES; do not peel.
1 Cut potatoes into thick wedges; dry with paper towels. Heat oil in deep heavy-based pan. Gently lower potato wedges into moderately hot oil. Cook for 4 minutes or until tender and lightly browned. Carefully remove from oil with a slotted spoon. Drain on paper towels.
2 Sift flour into large bowl; make a well in the centre. Add egg and beer. Using a wooden spoon, stir until just combined and smooth. Dust fish fillets in plain flour; shake off excess. Add fish fillets to batter, toss until well coated. Remove fish from batter, draining off excess batter.
3 Working with 1 piece of fish at a time, gently lower into moderately hot oil. Cook for 2 minutes or until golden and crisp and cooked through. Carefully remove from oil with slotted spoon. Drain on paper towels; keep warm.

Return potato wedges to moderately hot oil. Cook for another 2 minutes or until golden brown and crisp. Remove from oil with slotted spoon. Drain on paper towels. Sprinkle with spice salt, to taste. Serve immediately with fish and tartare sauce. If desired, serve with wedges of lemon and dill.

COOK'S FILE

Storage time: Cook fish and potato wedges just before serving.
Hint: Beer can be fizzy or flat.
Note: Old potatoes can be used instead of pontiac potatoes. Be sure to wash them well if you don't peel them. Spice salt is available from supermarkets.
Variation: Serve with sour cream and sweet chilli sauce instead of tartare sauce.

TUNA MORNAY

Preparation time: 25 minutes
Total cooking time: 20–25 minutes
Serves 4–6

425 g (15 oz) can tuna in oil,
    drained
1 tablespoon lemon juice
30 g (1 oz) butter
1 red onion, diced
2 sticks celery, chopped
440 g (1 lb) can cream of
    asparagus soup
80 ml (1/3 cup) milk
80 g (1 cup) fresh breadcrumbs
125 g (1/2 cup) grated Cheddar
    cheese
1 tablespoon chopped parsley

➤ PREHEAT OVEN to 180°C (350°F/
Gas 4). Grease a 1-litre (4 cup) ovenproof dish.
1 Combine tuna, lemon juice and
freshly ground black pepper in a
bowl. Spread evenly over base of
prepared dish.
2 Heat a frying pan over medium
heat. Melt butter, add onion. Stir for
5 minutes or until onion softens. Add
celery. Pour in soup and stir until
combined. Add milk. When mixture is
simmering, remove from heat and
pour over the tuna. Sprinkle combined
breadcrumbs, cheese and parsley
over the top. Bake, uncovered, for
15 minutes or until the cheese has
melted and top is golden. Serve hot.

COOK'S FILE

Note: This dish does not need added
salt.
Variations: Substitute 500 g (1 lb 2 oz)
boned white fish fillets for tuna.
   For a heartier meal, 350 g (12 oz)
cooked fettuccine or other pasta may
be stirred into the soup mixture.

TRADITIONAL GARLIC PRAWNS

Preparation time: 20 minutes
Total cooking time: 5 minutes
Serves 4

250 ml (1 cup) oil
60 g (2$\frac{1}{4}$ oz) butter, cut in
   4 even-sized cubes
8 garlic cloves, peeled
2 small red chillies, seeded and
   finely sliced
20 medium raw king prawns
   (shrimp), peeled, tails intact
2 tablespoons chopped parsley
baguette, for serving

➤ DIVIDE OIL among 4 fireproof dishes. Add 1 cube of butter to each dish. Prepare and heat barbecue.
1 Remove veins from prawns. Crush 2 cloves of garlic into each dish and divide chilli among the 4 dishes. Heat dishes on a barbecue flatplate until butter is very hot and bubbling. Add 5 prawns to each dish and cook for 3–4 minutes or until prawns are pink and cooked through. Sprinkle with parsley. Serve with the baguette.

1

COOK'S FILE

Variation: Prawns can be cooked in a pan on a hotplate. Heat oil with butter, garlic and chilli in a medium pan. When bubbling, add prawns and cook until pink. Preheat oven to 210°C (415°F/Gas 6–7). Heat 4 heatproof serving dishes in oven. Remove dishes from oven and place 5 prawns in each dish. Spoon some oil into each dish.

CHAR-GRILLED BABY OCTOPUS

Preparation time: 20 minutes
+ marinating
Total cooking time: 5 minutes
Serves 4

500 g (1 lb 2 oz) baby
    octopus
125 ml (¹/2 cup) olive oil
2 tablespoons lemon juice
2 tablespoons finely
    chopped coriander
    (cilantro)
1 tablespoon chilli sauce

➤ USING A sharp knife, cut head
from octopus; remove gut from inside.
1 Push the beak up and out of lower
section and discard. Wash octopus

thoroughly and dry on paper towels.
Place remaining ingredients in a bowl
and whisk until well combined. Add
octopus to bowl and stir well. Cover
and refrigerate for 2 hours or overnight.
Stir occasionally.
2 Heat grill or barbecue plate; brush
with oil to prevent sticking. Drain octopus; reserve marinade. Cook octopus
for 2–3 minutes on one side; turn

over and continue cooking for another
2–3 minutes. Brush with reserved marinade while cooking. Serve immediately.
Garnish with coriander, if desired.

COOK'S FILE

Storage time: Cover and refrigerate
cooked octopus for up to 2 days.
Hint: Octopus will toughen if it is
overcooked.

SMOKED FISH WITH WHITE SAUCE

Preparation time: 15 minutes
Total cooking time: 8 minutes
Serves 6

White Sauce
750 ml (3 cups) milk
1 onion, peeled and halved
1 clove
1 bay leaf
white pepper
60 g (2^1/4 oz) butter
40 g (^{1}/3 cup) plain (all-purpose) flour
20 g (^{1}/3 cup) chopped chives

1 kg (2 lb 4 oz) smoked cod or haddock fillets

➤ PREHEAT OVEN to 180°C (350°F/ Gas 4).

1 To make White Sauce: Place milk in a small pan with the onion, clove, bay leaf and white pepper. Heat slowly to a simmer. Remove from heat. Allow to stand for 3 minutes. Strain milk into a jug.

2 Heat butter in a medium pan; add flour. Stir constantly over low heat for 2–3 minutes or until lightly golden. Add strained milk gradually to pan, stirring until mixture is smooth. Stir constantly over medium heat for 8–10 minutes or until the sauce boils and thickens. Simmer for another minute; remove from heat. Season lightly with salt and pepper. Stir in chopped fresh chives.

3 Brush an ovenproof dish with melted butter or oil. Cut the fish fillets

into serving-sized pieces and place in prepared dish. Pour White Sauce over the fish. Bake for 10–15 minutes or until the fish is tender and flesh flakes at the thickest part. Serve with White Sauce on the top. Garnish with snipped chives, if desired.

COOK'S FILE

Note: Smoked fish is often very salty so if you want to make it less salty, combine 125 ml (^{1}/2 cup) milk and 125 ml (^{1}/2 cup) water in a bowl. Add fish and soak for several hours before cooking. Discard soaking liquid.
Variation: Instead of baking the fish, poach the fillets in 125 ml (^{1}/2 cup) milk and 125 ml (^{1}/2 cup) water, in a pan, until tender and flaking at the thickest part. Transfer to heated plates, pour White Sauce over fish.

SCALLOPS AND PRAWNS WITH CREAMY DILL SAUCE

Preparation time: 15 minutes
Total cooking time: 8 minutes
Serves 4

750 g (1 lb 10 oz) raw prawns (shrimp)
250 ml (1 cup) white wine
400 g (14 oz) scallops

8 spring onions (scallions), finely chopped
2 cloves garlic, crushed
2 tablespoons chopped dill
125 g (4^1/2 oz) butter, chopped
80 ml (^{1}/3 cup) thick (double/heavy) cream

➤ PEEL PRAWNS leaving tails intact, devein.

1 Place wine in medium pan, bring to the boil. Add prawns and scallops, simmer for 1 minute or until prawns

and scallops are just cooked through. Remove seafood with a slotted spoon.
2 Add spring onion, garlic and dill to wine, bring to the boil. Reduce heat to low, simmer, uncovered, for 2 minutes or until reduced by half.
3 Add butter gradually, whisking, until melted, after each addition. Add cream and seafood; stir until heated through. Garnish with dill, if desired.

COOK'S FILE

Hint: Delicious with boiled rice.

*Smoked Fish with White Sauce (top)
and Scallops and Prawns with Creamy Dill Sauce*

PERFECT *Prawns* IN MINUTES

STIR-FRIED GINGER PRAWNS

Peel and devein 1.25 kg (2 lb 12 oz) raw prawns (shrimp), leaving tails intact. Heat 2 tablespoons of oil in pan, add 2 crushed garlic cloves and 1 tablespoon grated fresh ginger, stir-fry over high heat for 1 minute. Add prawns, stir-fry over high heat for 1 minute. Add 60 ml ($1/4$ cup) dry sherry, 2 tablespoons lemon juice, 1 tablespoon soy sauce and 4 chopped spring onions (scallions). Stir-fry over high heat for 1 minute or until prawns are just tender. Serves 4.

BUTTERFLIED LEMON PRAWNS

Peel and devein 1 kg (2 lb 4 oz) raw prawns (shrimp), leaving tails intact. Cut prawns almost in half, lengthways, to form a butterfly; press firmly to flatten. Combine 150 g ($1^1/2$ cups) dried breadcrumbs, 2 teaspoons grated lemon zest and 1 tablespoon chopped parsley. Beat 1 egg with 1 tablespoon of water. Dip prawns into egg and allow excess to drain off. Roll in breadcrumb mixture, press firmly. Deep-fry in hot oil for 1 minute or until golden. Remove from oil. Sprinkle with salt and serve with lemon. Serves 4.

MOROCCAN PRAWNS

Peel and devein 1 kg (2 lb 4 oz) raw prawns (shrimp), leaving tails intact. Place 3 tablespoons coriander (cilantro) leaves and 3 tablespoons mint leaves in a food processor or blender with 2 tablespoons lemon juice, 1 crushed garlic clove, $1/2$ teaspoon ground paprika and $1/2$ teaspoon ground cumin. Blend for 20 seconds or until smooth. Transfer to a medium bowl, add prawns, stir until combined. Heat 2 tablespoons of oil in a heavy-based pan; add prawn mixture. Stir over high heat for 2 minutes or until prawns are just tender. Serve on a bed of rice. Serves 4.

PRAWN AND MINT SALAD WITH COCONUT DRESSING

Peel and devein 1 kg (2 lb 4 oz) cooked king prawns (shrimp), leaving tails intact. Combine prawns with 3 tablespoons sliced mint leaves and 2 tablespoons chopped coriander (cilantro). Place 80 ml ($1/3$ cup) coconut milk in jar with 1 tablespoon lemon juice,

MOROCCAN PRAWNS

STIR-FRIED GINGER PRAWNS

PRAWN AND MINT SALAD WITH COCONUT DRESSING

BUTTERFLIED LEMON PRAWNS

46

1 crushed garlic clove, 2 teaspoons Thai fish sauce, 1 teaspoon grated fresh ginger and 2 teaspoons soft brown sugar. Shake jar until combined; add to prawns, stir. Serve prawns on bed of mixed lettuce leaves. Serves 4.

CURRIED PRAWNS WITH VEGETABLES

Peel and devein 1 kg (2 lb 4 oz) raw king prawns (shrimp). Melt 60 g ($2^{1}/_{4}$ oz) butter in pan, add 2 red capsicums (peppers), cut into strips, and 2 thinly sliced carrots. Cook over low heat for 5 minutes or until vegetables are almost tender, stirring occasionally. Add 250 g (9 oz) broccoli florets, 250 ml (1 cup) coconut cream, 1 tablespoon curry paste and 250 ml (1 cup) water; bring to boil. Reduce heat and simmer, covered, for 5 minutes or until broccoli is tender. Add prawns and stir for 1 minute or until tender. Serve with rice. Serves 4.

PRAWN AND TOMATO SALAD WITH GINGER DRESSING

Peel and devein 1.25 kg (2 lb 12 oz) cooked medium prawns (shrimp). Cut 250 g (9 oz) asparagus spears in half. Drop into a pan of boiling water. Cook for 2 minutes or until just tender. Drain, rinse under cold water. Combine prawns and asparagus in large bowl with 2 tomatoes, cut into wedges, 200 g (7 oz) trimmed sugar snap peas and 4 chopped spring onions (scallions). Place 60 ml ($^{1}/_{4}$ cup) olive oil in a jar with 1 tablespoon lemon juice and 1 tablespoon grated fresh ginger. Shake for 10 seconds or until combined. Add to salad, stir until combined. Serves 4.

GLAZED STIR-FRIED PRAWNS

Peel and devein 1.25 kg (2 lb 12 oz) raw king prawns (shrimp). Place 60 ml ($^{1}/_{4}$ cup) red wine in a bowl with 2 tablespoons hoi sin sauce, 2 tablespoons honey and 2 crushed garlic cloves. Stir to combine. Add prawns and stir well. Heat 1 tablespoon of oil in a large pan, add 1 onion, cut in thin wedges, stir until softened. Add prawns and marinade. Stir over high heat for 1 minute or until prawns are tender. Serve with cellophane noodles. Garnish with herbs. Serves 4.

CURRIED PRAWNS WITH VEGETABLES

PRAWN AND TOMATO SALAD WITH GINGER DRESSING

GLAZED STIR-FRIED PRAWNS

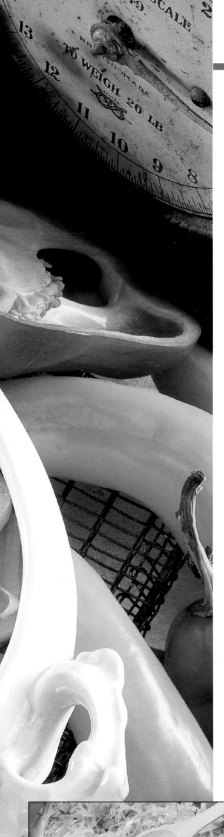

Magic MEAT MEALS

BEEF AND VEGETABLE BAKE

Preparation time: 35 minutes
Total cooking time: 40 minutes
Serves 4

30 g (1 oz) butter
750 g (1 lb 10 oz) potatoes,
    peeled, very thinly sliced
2 small leeks, sliced or
    2 onions, thinly sliced
20 g ($^3/4$ oz) butter, extra
1 red capsicum (pepper), sliced
1 tablespoon oil
750 g (1 lb 10 oz) lean minced
    (ground) beef
250 ml (1 cup) puréed tomato
80 ml ($^1/3$ cup) cream
grated Cheddar cheese, optional

➤ PREHEAT OVEN to 180°C (350°F/ Gas 4).
1 Melt butter in a large pan and add potato. Cook over medium–high heat, turning occasionally, for 5 minutes or until tender. Remove from pan. Add leek or onion to pan and stir for 3–5 minutes or until soft. Remove from pan. Add extra butter and capsicum; cook for 3–5 minutes or until softened; remove from pan.
2 Heat oil in pan; add beef. Cook over high heat for 5–10 minutes or until meat is well browned and all the liquid has evaporated. Use a fork to break up any lumps of beef as it cooks. Add puréed tomato and cream to pan; season with salt and pepper. Stir until combined.
3 Transfer mince mixture to 1.5-litre (6 cup) ovenproof dish. Top with combined potato, leek and capsicum. Sprinkle with cheese, if desired. Bake for 30 minutes or until potato is brown.

COOK'S FILE

Storage time: This dish can be made a day in advance. Store, covered with plastic wrap, in refrigerator.
Note: Potato is sliced and cooked before placing over mince so that it will be cooked properly.

2

3

GLAZED HONEY PORK RIBS

Preparation time: 10 minutes
 + marinating
Total cooking time: 45 minutes
Serves 4

115 g (¹/₃ cup) honey
80 ml (¹/₃ cup) plum sauce
80 ml (¹/₃ cup) cold, strong tea
2 tablespoons soy sauce
1 tablespoon grated fresh
  ginger
2 cloves garlic, crushed
¹/₂ teaspoon Chinese five-spice
  powder
1.5 kg (3 lb 5 oz) pork ribs

➤ PLACE ALL ingredients, except pork ribs, in a jug. Stir well to combine.

1 Place pork in a shallow non-metallic dish and pour on marinade. Brush to coat thoroughly. Cover and refrigerate overnight or several hours.

2 Preheat oven to 180°C (350°F/ Gas 4). Drain pork, reserve marinade. Place pork on a rack in a large baking dish. Bake for 45 minutes or until tender and golden. Turn pork occasionally and brush with reserved marinade during cooking. Garnish with shredded spring onion (scallions).

COOK'S FILE

Storage time: Pork can be marinated a day in advance. Store, covered, in refrigerator. Cook just before serving.

PORK STEAKS WITH ORANGE ROSEMARY SAUCE

Preparation time: 10 minutes
Total cooking time: 10 minutes
Serves 4

1 teaspoon grated orange zest
2 tablespoons orange juice
2 tablespoons olive oil
1 tablespoon seeded mustard
2 teaspoons chopped
   rosemary
2 teaspoons Worcestershire
   sauce
4 pork butterfly steaks

➤ IN A SMALL bowl, combine orange zest and juice, oil, mustard, rosemary and Worcestershire sauce.

1 Place pork medallions on lightly oiled griller (broiler) tray; brush with orange mixture. Cook under high heat for 5 minutes on each side or until cooked through, turning once. Brush medallions occasionally with orange mixture during cooking. Serve with fine strips of orange zest and salad greens, if desired.

COOK'S FILE

Storage time: Orange mixture can be made several hours in advance. Store, covered, in refrigerator. Cook medallions just before serving.
Variation: Pork schnitzels are also suitable for this recipe.

LAMB CHOPS WITH TOMATO-MINT RELISH

Preparation time: 5 minutes
Total cooking time: 20 minutes
Serves 4

2 large tomatoes
1 tablespoon oil
1 onion, finely chopped
2 teaspoons soft brown sugar
1 tablespoon red wine vinegar
1 tablespoon finely chopped mint

8 lamb loin chops

► USING A SHARP KNIFE, cut a small cross on bottom of each tomato.
1 Plunge into boiling water for 30 seconds, then into chilled water for a minute. Peel skin down from the cross. Chop tomatoes finely. Heat oil in a small pan. Add onion and cook over low heat for 5 minutes. Add tomato, sugar and vinegar; simmer for 10 minutes, stirring occasionally.
2 Add mint; stir. Serve relish warm or cold with chops.
3 Place chops on cold, lightly oiled griller (broiler) tray, cook under high heat 2 minutes each side, turning once. For rare meat, cook for another minute each side. For medium and well-done meat, lower griller (broiler) tray or reduce heat, cook for another 2–3 minutes each side for medium and 4–6 minutes each side for well done. Garnish with a sprig of mint, if desired.

COOK'S FILE

Storage time: Sauce can be made up to 2 days before required. Store, covered, in refrigerator. Reheat just before serving.
Hint: Serve with mashed potato and steamed peas or beans.
Variation: Use any cut of lamb, such as leg chops or fillets, if preferred.

1

2

3

VEAL WITH TOMATO-OLIVE SAUCE

Preparation time: 15 minutes
Total cooking time: 25 minutes
Serves 4

4 large veal loin chops
40 g (¼ cup) chopped sundried tomatoes, 2 tablespoons oil reserved
1 tablespoon oil
1 onion, sliced
1 tablespoon chopped rosemary
1 large tomato, finely chopped
2 tablespoons tomato paste (purée)

375 ml (1½ cups) chicken stock
35 g (¼ cup) chopped black olives

► TRIM EXCESS fat and sinew from veal chops.
1 Heat oil, reserved from sundried tomatoes, in pan; add chops. Cook over medium–high heat for 2 minutes each side or until browned; remove from pan.
2 Heat oil in pan; add onion and rosemary. Stir over medium heat for 5 minutes or until soft. Add finely chopped tomato, tomato paste and chicken stock; bring to the boil. Reduce heat to low and cover pan. Simmer mixture for 10 minutes or until sauce has reduced and thickened.
3 Return chops to pan. Add chopped sundried tomato and chopped olives. Simmer for 5 minutes or until chops are tender.

COOK'S FILE

Storage time: This recipe can be cooked a day in advance and stored, covered, in refrigerator. Reheat gently just before serving.
Hints: Use very ripe tomatoes for the best flavour when making this sauce.
Lamb chops or fillets can be used with this sauce.
May be served with boiled white or brown rice and steamed broccoli and baby carrots.

1

2

3

Lamb Chops with Tomato-mint Relish (top) and
Veal with Tomato-olive Sauce

LAMB CUTLETS WITH TANGY GARLIC AND THYME SAUCE

Preparation time: 10 minutes
Total cooking time: 10 minutes
Serves 2

2 tablespoons oil
4 lamb cutlets
60 ml (¹/4 cup) white wine
80 ml (¹/3 cup) thick
    (double/heavy) cream
4 cloves garlic, crushed
1 tablespoon chopped thyme

➤ PLACE OIL in large frying pan.
1 Trim excess fat and sinew from lamb cutlets. Heat oil, add chops to pan. Cook over high heat 3 minutes each side or until brown, turning once. Remove from pan; drain off excess fat.
2 Add wine, cream, garlic and chopped thyme to pan; bring to the boil. Reduce heat to low, simmer for 2 minutes or until liquid is reduced by half. Return drained chops to pan, simmer for 2 minutes or until chops are tender. Garnish with thyme, if desired.

COOK'S FILE

Variation: Use lamb loin or chump chops. Trim off any excess fat.

54

FILLET STEAK WITH PEPPER CHEESE SAUCE

Preparation time: 5 minutes
Total cooking time: 5–10 minutes
Serves 4

4 large beef fillet steaks

Pepper Cheese Sauce
**2 tablespoons oil
1 small leek, thinly sliced or
    1 onion, thinly sliced
250 ml (1 cup) chicken stock
125 g (4$^{1}/_{2}$ oz) pepper cheese,
    cut in small cubes**

► PLACE STEAKS on cold, lightly
oiled griller (broiler) tray.
1 Cook under high heat for 2 minutes
each side to seal, turning once. For
rare meat, cook for another minute
each side. For medium and well-done
meat, lower griller (broiler) tray
or reduce heat. Cook for another
2–3 minutes each side for medium and
4–6 minutes each side for well-done.
**2 To make Pepper Cheese
Sauce:** Heat oil in a medium pan, add
leek or onion. Stir over medium heat
for 3 minutes or until tender. Add
stock and cheese, stir for 1 minute or
until cheese has melted and sauce has
thickened. Serve with steaks.

COOK'S FILE

Hint: Serve with steamed butter beans,
thinly sliced carrots and halved yellow
and green squash. Use herbs to garnish.
Variation: This sauce is delicious
with grilled lamb, pork and veal chops.

1

2

CREAMY TOMATO MEATLOAF

Preparation time: 10 minutes
+ refrigeration
Total cooking time: 1 hour
Serves 6

750 g (1 lb 10 oz) minced
  (ground) beef
170 g ($^2/_3$ cup) sour cream
50 g (1$^3/_4$ oz) tomato soup mix
1 onion, finely chopped
2 cloves garlic, crushed
3 teaspoons ground paprika
1 teaspoon chopped red chilli

➤ PREHEAT OVEN to 180°C (350°F/
Gas 4). Lightly grease a 21 x 14 x 7 cm
(8$^1/_2$ x 5$^1/_2$ x 2$^3/_4$ inch) loaf tin, line
base and sides with paper.

1 Place beef in a large bowl with
remaining ingredients and mix until
well combined.

2 Press mixture firmly into prepared
loaf tin. Bake for 1 hour or until well
browned and firm in the centre. Turn
out of tin, serve sliced. Serve with
salad, if desired.

COOK'S FILE

Storage time: Meatloaf may be
served hot or cold. If serving hot, cook
just before serving. If serving cold,
meat loaf can be cooked up to 2 days
before required. Store, covered, in
refrigerator.

Variation: This recipe can be made
with pork and veal mince.

VEAL PARMIGIANA

Preparation time: 15 minutes
+ refrigeration
Total cooking time: 25 minutes
Serves 4

4 thin slices veal
plain (all-purpose) flour, for
    coating
1 egg, lightly beaten
dry breadcrumbs, for coating
30 g (1 oz) butter
60 ml (¹/4 cup) oil
160 g (²/3 cup) bottled chunky
    tomato pasta sauce

50 g (¹/2 cup) grated Parmesan
    cheese
75 g (¹/2 cup) grated mozzarella
    cheese

➤ PAT VEAL dry with paper towels.
1 Place flour on a plate, egg in a bowl, and breadcrumbs on another plate. Coat veal with flour, dip in egg and then coat with breadcrumbs. Refrigerate for approximately 1 hour.
2 Preheat oven to 180°C (350°F/Gas 4). Brush a medium-sized ovenproof dish with oil. Heat butter and oil in a large frying pan. Add veal to pan and cook for 2–3 minutes each side or until golden. Drain on paper towels.

3 Place in a single layer in prepared dish, spoon tomato pasta sauce over and sprinkle with combined cheeses. Bake uncovered for 20–25 minutes or until golden. Serve immediately, with salad, if desired.

COOK'S FILE

Storage time: Recipe may be completed, up to baking stage, several hours ahead, covered, and refrigerated. Cook just before serving. Dish may also be frozen, without cheeses, for up to 1 month. Sprinkle cheeses on top just before cooking.
Variation: Instead of mozzarella, use Cheddar cheese.

BEEF CURRY WITH FRESH HERBS

Preparation time: 10 minutes
Total cooking time: 1 hour 45 minutes
Serves 4

1 tablespoon oil
600 g (1 lb 5 oz) round steak, cut into cubes
2 onions, chopped
1 tablespoon curry paste
500 ml (2 cups) water or beef stock
2 tablespoons chopped mint
2 tablespoons chopped coriander (cilantro)
90 g (¹/₃ cup) plain yoghurt

➤ HEAT OIL in heavy-based pan.
1 Add beef cubes, cook in batches over medium–high heat for 2 minutes or until well browned on all sides. Return all meat to pan.
2 Add onion, stir for 2 minutes or until brown. Add curry paste, stir for 1 minute. Add water or beef stock, bring to the boil. Reduce heat to low and cook, covered, 1–1¹/₂ hours or until meat is tender and liquid is reduced and thickened. Stir occasion-ally during cooking. Add chopped mint, coriander and yoghurt; stir until combined. Garnish with a sprig of fresh herbs, if desired.

COOK'S FILE

Storage time: Curry can be cooked up to 3 days before required. Store, covered, in refrigerator.
Hint: Serve with steamed basmati rice and curried vegetables.

INDIVIDUAL BEEF WELLINGTONS

Preparation time: 20 minutes
 + refrigeration
Total cooking time: 15 minutes
Serves 4

4 beef eye fillet steaks,
    approximately 4 cm
    ($1^1/2$ inches) thick
20 g ($3/4$ oz) butter
1 tablespoon oil
100 g ($3^1/2$ oz) pâté
100 g ($3^1/2$ oz) button
    mushrooms, finely sliced
4 sheets puff pastry
1 egg yolk

➤ TIE STRING AROUND steaks to keep round shape. Heat butter and oil in heavy-based frying pan. Add steaks and cook over high heat 2 minutes. Turn; cook for another 2 minutes or until done to your liking. Remove from heat; cover and allow to cool.

1 Remove string from steaks. Spread a layer of pâté on one side of each steak. Press mushrooms on pâté. Place steak, mushroom-side down on sheet of pastry. Trim and fit pastry to form a neat parcel with folds on the underside. Seal with combined egg yolk and 2 teaspoons water.

2 Use pastry scraps to decorate top of the parcel. Make 2 slits on top of pastry. Brush with egg mixture. Repeat with remaining steaks. Refrigerate parcels for about 1 hour. Preheat oven to 210°C (415°F/ Gas 6–7). Bake for 5 minutes. Reduce heat to 180°C (350°F/Gas 4) and bake for another 8–10 minutes or until pastry is cooked. Serve with baked or steamed vegetables of your choice.

LAMB FILLETS WITH BEAN AND ROSEMARY PUREE

Preparation time: 10 minutes
Total cooking time: 5–10 minutes
Serves 4

1 tablespoon oil
4 small lamb fillets

Bean and Rosemary Purée
400 g (14 oz) can cannellini
  beans, drained
80 ml (¹/₃ cup) olive oil
3 teaspoons chopped
  rosemary
2 teaspoons lemon juice
¹/₂ teaspoon ground
  paprika
2 cloves garlic,
  crushed

➤ HEAT OIL in large frying pan; add lamb fillets.

1 Cook over high heat 2–3 minutes each side to seal, turning once. For rare meat, cook another minute each side. For medium and well-done fillets, reduce heat to medium. Continue cooking another 2–3 minutes each side for medium fillets and 4–6 minutes each side for well-done. Remove from pan; drain on paper towels. Cover, keep warm for 5 minutes. Cut lamb fillets into thin diagonal slices. Serve with Bean and Rosemary Purée.

2 To make Bean and Rosemary Purée: Combine beans, oil, rosemary, lemon juice, paprika, garlic, salt and pepper in food processor or blender. Blend 30 seconds or until smooth. Transfer purée to small pan; stir over medium heat 1 minute or until heated through. May be served with pan-fried onion slices and steamed vegetables.

STEAK WITH MUSHROOM AND WINE SAUCE

Preparation time: 10 minutes
Total cooking time: 15 minutes
Serves 4

2 rump steaks, 3 cm
    (1¼ inches) thick
2 teaspoons butter
1 tablespoon oil
3 spring onions (scallions),
    finely chopped
125 g (4½ oz) button
    mushrooms, finely sliced
3 teaspoons cornflour
    (cornstarch)
250 ml (1 cup) red wine
15 g (¼ cup) chopped parsley

➤ TRIM ALL fat from steaks; cut each steak in half. Heat butter and oil in a heavy-based frying pan.

1 Cook steaks over high heat for 2 minutes; turn over and cook for another 2 minutes or until done to your liking. Remove steaks from pan, cover and keep warm. Add spring onion to pan, stir for 3 minutes, add mushrooms and stir for 3 minutes or until mushrooms are soft.

2 Combine cornflour with 2 tablespoons of the wine to form a smooth paste. Stir into remaining wine and add all at once to the mushroom mixture. Cook until mixture boils and thickens. Stir in parsley. Place steaks on serving dishes. Spoon sauce over fillets; serve immediately. Serve with salad greens or steamed vegetables.

SUPER *Stir-fries* IN MINUTES

THAI LAMB WITH VEGETABLES

Heat 60 ml (^{1}/4 cup) oil in wok or heavy-based pan. Add 500 g (1 lb 2 oz) thinly sliced lamb fillets, cook over high heat until browned; remove from pan. Add to pan 4 zucchini (courgettes), cut into straws and 400 g (14 oz) snowpeas (mangetout); stir over high heat 2 minutes or until tender. Return lamb to pan with 125 ml (^{1}/2 cup) chicken stock, 3 tablespoons chopped coriander (cilantro), 2 tablespoons chopped mint, 1 tablespoon fish sauce, ^{1}/2–1 teaspoon chopped chilli and 1 teaspoon garam masala. Stir for 30 seconds or until heated through. Sprinkle with lemon and lime juice. Serves 4.

SWEET AND SOUR PORK

Heat 2 tablespoons oil in wok or heavy-based pan; add 600 g (1 lb 5 oz) cubed pork. Cook over high heat 3 minutes or until brown, remove from pan. Heat 1 tablespoon oil in pan, add 1 onion, cut into wedges, and 1 green capsicum (pepper), cut into squares, stir-fry over medium heat for 2 minutes. Return pork to pan with 440 g (1 lb) can undrained pineapple pieces, 60 ml (^{1}/4 cup) tomato sauce and 2 tablespoons white vinegar. Stir over medium heat 2 minutes or until pork and vegetables are tender and sauce has thickened. Serve on rice. Serves 4.

LAMB WITH PLUM SAUCE

Heat 2 tablespoons oil in wok or heavy-based pan; add 500 g (1 lb 2 oz) lamb, cut into thin strips. Stir over high heat 2 minutes or until

THAI LAMB WITH VEGETABLES

brown, remove from pan. Add 1 onion, cut into wedges, and 2 teaspoons grated fresh ginger; stir 2 minutes or until onion is tender. Add 250 g (9 oz) sugar snap peas, stir 1 minute. Return lamb to pan with 180 g (2 cups) bean sprouts, 125 ml (^{1}/2 cup) plum sauce; stir over heat 1 minute or until heated through. Serve on a bed of noodles. Serves 4.

STIR-FRIED PORK WITH SPINACH

Heat 2 tablespoons oil in wok or heavy-based pan; add 500 g (1 lb 2 oz) pork fillet, thinly sliced. Stir over high heat 2 minutes. Add 2 crushed garlic cloves, 1 tablespoon balsamic vinegar, 1 tablespoon soy sauce and 2 teaspoons grated ginger; stir 30 seconds. Remove from heat; add 500 g (1 lb 2 oz) English spinach. Stir 30 seconds or until spinach is slightly wilted. Serves 4.

LAMB WITH PLUM SAUCE

STIR-FRIED PORK WITH SPINACH

SWEET AND SOUR PORK

STIR-FRIED BEEF WITH BOK CHOY

Heat 2 tablespoons oil in wok or heavy-based pan; add 2 tablespoons soy sauce, 1 crushed garlic clove and 500 g (1 lb 2 oz) fillet steak, cut into thin strips. Cook over high heat until browned, remove from pan. Add 6 spring onions (scallions), cut into short lengths, 180 g (4 cups) chopped bok choy (pak choi) and 180 g (2 cups) bean sprouts, stir over high heat 30 seconds. Blend 2 teaspoons cornflour (cornstarch) with 2 tablespoons black bean sauce and 375 ml (1^1/$_2$ cups) chicken stock. Add to pan with beef; stir over high heat 1 minute. Drizzle with sweet chilli sauce. Serves 4.

STIR-FRIED LAMB WITH LEEKS

Trim 12 lamb fillets of excess fat and sinew. Slice diagonally across grain into thin strips. Combine lamb in bowl with 2 tablespoons soy sauce, 2 tablespoons dry sherry and 1 tablespoon grated fresh ginger. Allow to stand 5 minutes. Drain; reserve marinade. Heat 2 tablespoons sesame oil in wok or heavy-based pan and add 2 small, thinly sliced leeks or 2 sliced onions; stir over high heat for 1 minute or until browned. Remove from pan. Add lamb to pan; cook over high heat 2 minutes until browned but not cooked through; remove from pan. Add 400 g (14 oz) medium mushroom caps, sliced, and stir over high heat 1 minute. Add 250 ml (1 cup) chicken stock, reserved marinade, lamb and leeks, stir over heat for 1 minute or until heated through. Serves 4.

PORK WITH OYSTER MUSHROOMS

Heat 1 tablespoon oil in wok or heavy-based frying pan. Add 1 onion, cut into wedges, 2 crushed garlic cloves, ^{1}/$_2$ teaspoon black pepper. Stir 1 minute; remove from pan. Heat 1 tablespoon oil, stir in 500 g (1 lb 2 oz) thinly sliced pork for 1 minute, remove from pan. Add 150 g (5^1/$_2$ oz) halved oyster mushrooms, 415 g (14 oz) can baby sweet corn, 1 tablespoon oyster sauce, 2 teaspoons soy sauce and 2 teaspoons sesame oil. Stir over heat 1 minute. Return all ingredients to pan; heat through. Serve with flat noodles and garnish with herbs, if desired. Serves 4.

TERIYAKI BEEF AND BROCCOLI

Heat 1 tablespoon oil in a wok or heavy-based pan. Add 400 g (14 oz) broccoli florets, 1 crushed garlic clove and 3 spring onions (scallions), cut into short lengths. Stir for 2 minutes; remove from pan. Heat an extra tablespoon of oil in pan; add 500 g (1 lb 2 oz) beef, cut into thin strips; stir for 1 minute. Return vegetables to pan and add 2 tablespoons teriyaki sauce, 1 tablespoon sweet sherry and 1 teaspoon sesame oil. Stir 1 minute to combine sauce with meat and vegetables. Serves 4.

STIR-FRIED BEEF WITH BOK CHOY

STIR-FRIED LAMB WITH LEEKS

PORK WITH OYSTER MUSHROOMS

TERIYAKI BEEF AND BROCCOLI

Chicken IN A FLASH

ASIAN GRILLED CHICKEN WITH BOK CHOY

Preparation time: 10 minutes
 + marinating
Total cooking time: 15–20 minutes
Serves 4

115 g (¹/₃ cup) honey
60 ml (¹/₄ cup) oil
1 tablespoon grated fresh
   ginger
2 teaspoons sweet chilli sauce
1¹/₂ teaspoons Chinese
   five-spice powder
8 chicken thighs
500 g (1 lb 2 oz) bok choy
   (pak choi)
250 ml (1 cup) chicken stock

➤ COMBINE HONEY, oil, ginger, chilli sauce and five-spice in a small bowl.
1 Place chicken thighs in a large non-metal dish. Pour honey mixture over chicken thighs. Cover and refrigerate for several hours or overnight. Drain chicken and reserve marinade.
2 Place chicken on cold, lightly oiled griller (broiler) tray; brush with reserved marinade. Cook under medium-high heat for 15–20 minutes or until tender, brushing with honey mixture several times during cooking. Turn chicken occasionally.
3 Meanwhile, rinse bok choy, pat dry and trim off excess stems. Place chicken stock in a medium pan and bring to the boil. Add bok choy; cover pan. Reduce heat to low and simmer for 3 minutes or until tender. Drain bok choy and arrange on serving plates. Place cooked chicken on top.

COOK'S FILE

Storage time: Cook chicken just before serving.
Note: Bok choy is a green leafy vegetable, similar to spinach. It is available from most fruit and vegetable stores. However, if unavailable, English spinach or silverbeet (Swiss chard) may be used instead.

CHICKEN WITH SPRING ONION AND MUSTARD SAUCE

Preparation time: 15 minutes
Total cooking time: 15 minutes
Serves 4

8 chicken thigh fillets
60 g ($^1/_4$ cup) Dijon mustard
2 tablespoons oil
6 spring onions (scallions),
   chopped
1 tablespoon plain (all-purpose)
   flour
375 ml ($1^1/_2$ cups) chicken
   stock
1 tablespoon chopped thyme

➤ CUT CHICKEN fillets in half, place in a medium bowl. Add mustard and toss until chicken is well coated.
1 Heat oil in a large pan; add chicken in a single layer. Cook over high heat for 5 minutes or until golden brown, turning once. Remove from pan.
2 Add spring onion to pan, stir over medium heat for 1 minute. Add flour to pan, stir for 1 minute. Add stock and thyme. Stir until smooth; bring to boil.
3 Return chicken to pan, reduce heat to low. Cook, uncovered, turning occasionally, for 10 minutes or until chicken is tender. Serve chicken with sauce spooned over the top.

COOK'S FILE

Storage time: This dish can be cooked a day before required. Store, covered, in refrigerator. Reheat gently just before serving.

GRILLED CHICKEN BREAST WITH BARBECUE GLAZE

Preparation time: 10 minutes
+ marinating
Total cooking time: 10 minutes
Serves 4

80 ml (¹/₃ cup) barbecue sauce
1 tablespoon honey
60 g (¹/₄ cup) mayonnaise
2 cloves garlic, crushed
2 teaspoons grated fresh ginger
4 chicken breast fillets

➤ COMBINE BARBECUE sauce, honey, mayonnaise, garlic and ginger in a medium bowl.

1 Add chicken fillets to bowl, toss until well coated. Cover and refrigerate for several hours or overnight.
2 Place chicken on cold, lightly oiled griller (broiler) tray. Cook, brushing occasionally with remaining marinade, under high heat 5–8 minutes. Turn; cook other side 5–8 minutes or until chicken is tender. Slice chicken for serving. Serve with a crisp green salad.

COOK'S FILE

Variations: The glaze in this recipe is suitable for other cuts of chicken such as thigh fillets and wings.

Barbecue chicken instead of grilling.

1

2

CHICKEN WITH LEMON AND BASIL SAUCE

Preparation time: 10 minutes
Total cooking time: 10 minutes
Serves 4

55 g (²/₃ cup) fresh breadcrumbs
60 ml (¼ cup) olive oil
60 ml (¼ cup) lemon juice
15 g (¼ cup) chopped basil
3 cloves garlic, crushed
1 teaspoon sugar
8 chicken thigh fillets
1 tablespoon olive oil, extra

➤ PLACE BREADCRUMBS in a food processor or blender.

1 Add oil, lemon juice, basil, garlic and sugar. Blend for 20 seconds or until smooth. Transfer to medium pan and stir gently over low heat 2 minutes or until heated through. Serve with chicken.
2 Trim chicken of excess fat and sinew. Place on cold, lightly oiled griller (broiler) tray. Brush chicken with oil and cook under medium–high heat 5 minutes each side or until tender. Serve with sauce. Garnish with basil.

COOK'S FILE

Storage time: Sauce can be made several hours before required. Store, with plastic wrap pressed down over surface of sauce, in refrigerator.
Variation: Chicken can be fried or baked instead of grilled, if preferred.

SATAY CHICKEN

Preparation time: 15 minutes
Total cooking time: 10–15 minutes
Serves 4

**750 g (1 lb 10 oz) chicken thigh
  fillets**
1 tablespoon oil
1 onion, chopped
**125 g (¹/₂ cup) crunchy peanut
  butter**
80 ml (¹/₃ cup) chicken stock
2 cloves garlic, crushed
2 tablespoons fruit chutney
3 teaspoons red curry paste
2 teaspoons soy sauce

➤ TRIM CHICKEN thigh fillets of excess fat and sinew. Cut chicken into 2.5 cm (1 inch) cubes. Soak wooden skewers in water.

1 Heat oil in pan; add onion and stir until soft. Transfer to food processor or blender. Add remaining ingredients. Process for 1 minute or until smooth.

2 Thread chicken onto skewers. Place skewers on cold, lightly oiled griller (broiler) tray; brush with peanut mixture. Cook under high heat for 5 minutes on each side or until tender, brushing with peanut mixture several times during cooking. Place remaining peanut mixture in a small pan, stir over medium heat for 3–5 minutes or until heated through. Serve with chicken skewers.

COOK'S FILE

Storage time: Chicken can be marinated in refrigerator overnight.

CHICKEN WITH MUSTARD AND CHEESE

Preparation time: 20 minutes
Total cooking time: 10 minutes
Serves 4

4 chicken breast fillets
4 slices leg ham
1 tablespoon Dijon mustard
30 g ($^1/4$ cup) finely grated
   Cheddar cheese
40 g ($^1/2$ cup) fresh or dry
   breadcrumbs

plain (all-purpose) flour, for
   dusting
1 egg, lightly beaten
60 ml ($^1/4$ cup) oil

➤ PREHEAT oven to 180° C (350°F/Gas 4).
1 Place chicken fillets under-side up on work surface. Flatten slightly to an even thickness. Top with ham, trim ham to fit. Spread with mustard. Fold chicken fillet over to enclose ham.
2 Combine cheese and breadcrumbs in a bowl. Dust chicken pieces lightly in flour; shake off excess. Dip chicken in egg; coat with breadcrumb mixture, press on firmly.
3 Heat oil in a large frying pan. Cook chicken pieces over medium heat for 3–4 minutes each side or until golden brown. Drain on paper towels. Garnish with a sprig of thyme.

COOK'S FILE

Storage time: Chicken can be assembled several hours ahead. Store, covered, in refrigerator. Cook just before serving.
Hints: Leg ham off the bone will give the best flavour for this recipe.

CHICKEN DRUMSTICKS CHASSEUR

Preparation time: 10 minutes
Total cooking time: 45 minutes
Serves 4

60 g ($2^1/4$ oz) butter
8 chicken drumsticks
400 g (14 oz) button
   mushrooms, chopped
2 onions, sliced
1 clove garlic, crushed
2 tablespoons plain (all-purpose)
   flour
500 ml (2 cups) chicken stock
80 ml ($^1/3$ cup) good-quality red
   wine

90 g (1/3 cup) tomato paste
   (purée)

➤ MELT 40 g ($1^1/2$ oz) butter in large pan; add drumsticks in a single layer.
1 Cook over medium heat, turning occasionally, for 4 minutes or until browned. Remove from pan. Drain on paper towels. Add mushrooms to pan, stir over medium heat until well browned. Remove from pan.
2 Add remaining butter, onion and garlic to pan, stir over medium heat for 5–10 minutes or until golden. Add flour to pan, stir over medium heat for 1 minute. Add stock, wine and tomato paste. Stir over medium heat until smooth, bring to the boil.
3 Return chicken and mushrooms to pan. Reduce heat to low; cover pan. Cook for 15 minutes. Uncover; simmer, stirring occasionally, for another 15 minutes, or until chicken is tender. If liquid reduces too much, add a little more stock or wine. Season with salt and pepper before serving. May be garnished with chopped fresh thyme.

COOK'S FILE

Storage time: This dish can be cooked the day before required. Store, covered, in refrigerator. Reheat just before serving.
Note: Boiled rice or mashed potato make a suitable accompaniment.
Variations: Any cut of chicken, such as thigh fillets or breasts, can be used for this recipe.

*Chicken with Mustard and Cheese (top)
and Chicken Drumsticks Chasseur*

CHICKEN AND POTATO SALAD

Preparation time: 20 minutes
Total cooking time: 10 minutes
Serves 6

1 barbecued chicken
750 g (1 lb 10 oz) small new
   potatoes, halved
60 ml (1/4 cup) olive oil
2 tablespoons tarragon
   vinegar
1 teaspoon French mustard
2 tablespoons chopped
   chives

➤ REMOVE MEAT from chicken, discard bones.
1 Cut or shred chicken into pieces; set aside. Cook potatoes in a large pan of boiling water until tender. Drain and cool slightly.
2 Place oil, vinegar and mustard in a small screw-top jar; shake until combined and season. Place chicken, potato and chives in large bowl. Pour dressing over and toss to combine. Serve warm or at room temperature.

Variations: Different chopped herbs may be used in place of chives. Try chopped coriander (cilantro), parsley or basil.

Steamed or fried chicken pieces, such as breasts or thighs, can be used instead of barbecued chicken. Cook, allow to cool, refrigerate before use.

TANDOORI CHICKEN AND VEGETABLE SKEWERS

Preparation time: 15 minutes
Total cooking time: 10 minutes
Serves 4

250 g (1 cup) plain yoghurt
2 cloves garlic, crushed
2 teaspoons grated fresh ginger
2 teaspoons ground turmeric
2 teaspoons garam masala
6 chicken thigh fillets, cut
    into 4 cm (1^{1}/$_{2}$ inch) cubes
1 red capsicum (pepper), cut into
    2.5 cm (1 inch) squares
1 onion, cut into thin wedges

➤ COMBINE YOGHURT in a small bowl with garlic, ginger, turmeric and garam masala. Set aside.

1 Thread chicken, capsicum and onion alternately onto soaked skewers. Brush yoghurt mixture lightly over skewers.

2 Place skewers on cold, lightly oiled griller (broiler) tray and cook, brushing with yoghurt mixture occasionally, under high heat for 5 minutes. Turn and cook, brushing again with yoghurt mixture, for 5 minutes or until chicken is tender. Serve with saffron rice, if desired.

COOK'S FILE

Storage time: Skewers can be prepared a day ahead. Store, covered, in refrigerator. Cook just before serving.

LEMON GARLIC CHICKEN

Preparation time: 5 minutes
  + marinating
Total cooking time: 1 hour
Serves 4

4 pieces chicken Maryland
  (leg quarter)
80 ml (1/3 cup) lemon juice
4 cloves garlic, crushed
60 g (2 1/4 oz) butter, melted
1 teaspoon ground paprika

➤ PLACE CHICKEN pieces in a non-metal dish.

1 Combine lemon juice, garlic, butter, paprika and pepper. Pour mixture over chicken. Cover and refrigerate for several hours or overnight.

2 Preheat oven to 180°C (350°F/ Gas 4). Transfer chicken to a baking dish. Bake, brushing occasionally with lemon mixture, for 1 hour or until chicken is tender and golden brown. Garnish with lemon wedges, if desired.

COOK'S FILE

Hint: Bottled lemon juice is available from supermarkets and delicatessens.
Variations: Other chicken pieces such as breasts or thighs may be used. Barbecue chicken instead of baking.

CHICKEN WITH CAPSICUM AND GARLIC

Preparation time: 10 minutes
Total cooking time: 25 minutes
Serves 4

60 ml (¹/₄ cup) olive oil
8 chicken thigh fillets, halved
2 onions, sliced
6 cloves garlic, crushed
4 bacon rashers, sliced
2 red capsicums (peppers), sliced
425 g (15 oz) can tomatoes
60 ml (¹/₄ cup) chicken stock

➤ HEAT OIL in pan; add chicken in single layer.

1 Cook over medium–high heat for 3 minutes each side or until golden. Remove from pan and drain on paper towels. Add onion, garlic and bacon to pan. Cook, stirring, for 3–5 minutes or until golden. Add capsicum, cook for another 3 minutes, stirring occasionally.

2 Add undrained, crushed tomato and stock to pan; bring to the boil. Reduce heat to low. Return chicken to pan and simmer, covered, for 15 minutes or until chicken is tender, stirring occasionally. Season with salt and pepper. Serve.

COOK'S FILE

Storage time: This dish can be cooked a day before required. Store, covered, in refrigerator.
Variation: Use 2 slices of prosciutto instead of bacon.

ROASTED MARYLANDS WITH SAGE AND PROSCIUTTO

Preparation time: 10 minutes
 + marinating
Total cooking time: 40 minutes
Serves 4

2 tablespoons oil
2 teaspoons seeded
  mustard
1 clove garlic, crushed
4 pieces chicken Maryland
  (leg quarter)
16 sage leaves
4 slices prosciutto

➤ COMBINE OIL, mustard, garlic and pepper in a small bowl.

1 Using a sharp knife, make diagonal cuts across the top of each chicken maryland. Place chicken in a non-metal dish. Brush oil mixture over chicken. Cover and refrigerate for several hours or overnight.

2 Preheat oven to 180°C (350°F/ Gas 4). Transfer chicken to large baking dish. Lay sage leaves over chicken Marylands. Cut prosciutto slices crossways in half, lay over the sage. Bake 40 minutes or until golden and tender.

COOK'S FILE

Hint: Delicious served with steamed carrots and beans or broccoli.

1

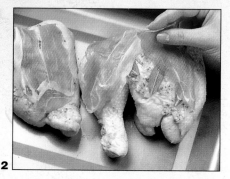

2

ROAST CHICKEN WITH FRESH HERB STUFFING

Preparation time: 20 minutes
+ 10 minutes standing
Total cooking time: 1 hour 30 minutes
Serves 4–6

3 slices wholegrain bread,
   crusts removed
3 spring onions (scallions),
   chopped
60 g (1 cup) chopped parsley
1 tablespoon chopped thyme
1 tablespoon chopped oregano
1 teaspoon grated lemon zest
1 egg, lightly beaten
1.4 kg (3 lb 4 oz) chicken
1 tablespoon oil

➤ PREHEAT OVEN to 180°C (350°F/ Gas 4).
1 Cut bread into small squares; place in a medium bowl. Add onion, herbs, lemon zest and egg. Mix well.
2 Remove giblets and excess fat from chicken. Wipe and pat dry chicken with paper towels. Spoon stuffing into chicken cavity; close cavity with a toothpick or skewer. Tie legs together with string. Place on roasting rack in a deep baking dish, brush with oil. Roast the chicken for 1 hour 25 minutes or until brown and tender. Remove from oven and leave, loosely covered with foil, in a warm place for 10 minutes. Remove toothpick and string before carving. Garnish with sprigs of fresh herbs and slices of lemon, if desired.

77

BRILLIANT BBQ *Chicken* IN MINUTES

CHICKEN WITH ALMONDS AND BASIL

Remove skin from a small, hot barbecued chicken. Shred meat; place in bowl. Place 60 g ($^1/_2$ cup) slivered almonds in pan, stir over high heat 2 minutes. Add 80 ml ($^1/_3$ cup) herb and garlic dressing and 2 teaspoons sweet chilli sauce, stir over heat 10 seconds. Add to chicken with 20 g ($^1/_3$ cup) chopped basil, stir. Serves 4.

STIR-FRIED CHICKEN, ASPARAGUS AND BEANS

Remove skin; shred meat of a barbecued chicken. Heat 2 tablespoons oil in heavy-based pan. Add 250 g (9 oz) halved green beans and 250 g (9 oz) halved asparagus spears, stir over medium heat 3 minutes or until tender. Add chicken, 250 g (9 oz) rocket (arugula) leaves, 1 tablespoon tarragon vinegar, 2 teaspoons seeded mustard and 2 tablespoons oil. Stir 1 minute. Serves 4.

CHICKEN AND COUSCOUS SALAD

Remove skin from half a barbecued chicken. Shred meat. Combine 230 g ($1^1/_4$ cups) instant couscous and 750 ml (3 cups) boiling water in bowl, stand 5 minutes until water is absorbed. Add chicken with 250 g (9 oz) halved cherry tomatoes, 1 sliced Lebanese (short) cucumber, 1 cup (60 g) chopped parsley, 4 chopped spring onions (scallions), 1 sliced avocado, and 125 ml ($^1/_2$ cup) French dressing; stir until combined. Serves 4.

MEDITERRANEAN CHICKEN SALAD

Remove skin from a small barbecued chicken. Shred meat. Combine with 200 g (7 oz) rocket (arugula), 250 g (9 oz) snowpeas (mangetout), 2 tomatoes, cut into wedges and 125 g ($4^1/_2$ oz) cubed feta. Whisk 125 ml ($^1/_2$ cup) French dressing, 60 g ($^1/_4$ cup) mayonnaise and 15 g ($^1/_4$ cup) chopped mint. Add to chicken. Serves 4.

CHICKEN WITH MANGO SAUCE

Combine 425 g (15 oz) drained can mangoes in food processor with 80 ml ($^1/_3$ cup) chicken stock, 90 g ($^1/_3$ cup) sour cream and 1 teaspoon curry powder. Blend 30 seconds or until smooth. Transfer to pan, add 20 g ($^1/_3$ cup) chopped chives, stir over heat 2 minutes. Cut a small, hot barbecued chicken into pieces. Serve with sauce and pasta. Serves 4.

CHICKEN WITH ALMONDS AND BASIL

STIR-FRIED CHICKEN, ASPARAGUS AND BEANS

CHICKEN AND COUSCOUS SALAD

MEDITERRANEAN CHICKEN SALAD

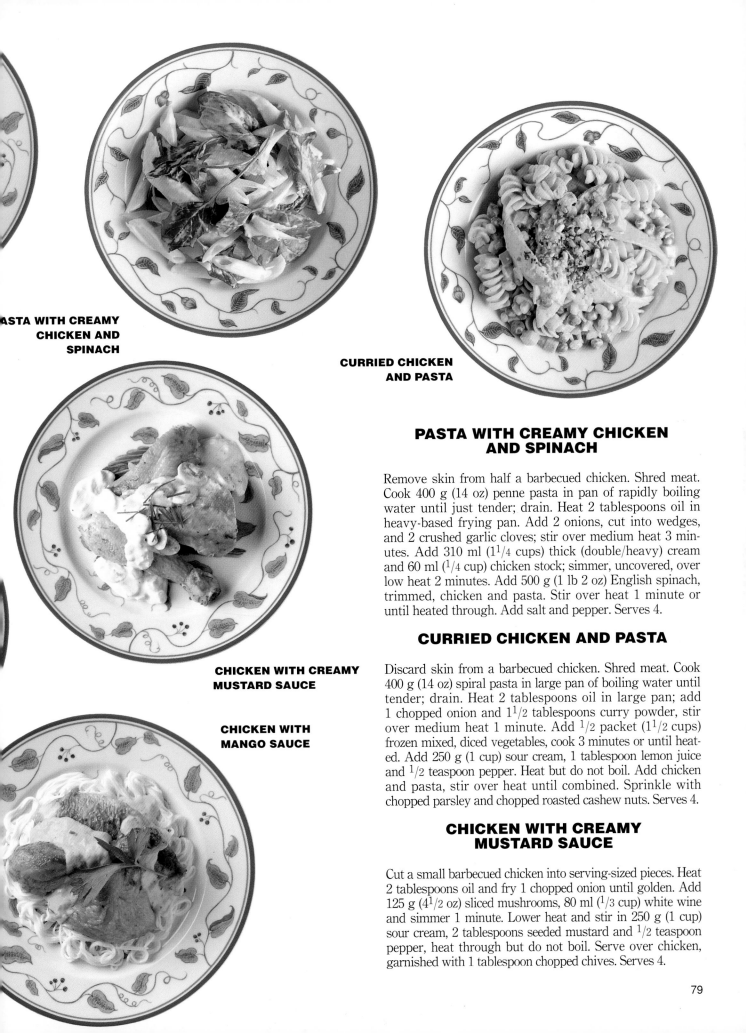

**PASTA WITH CREAMY
CHICKEN AND
SPINACH**

**CURRIED CHICKEN
AND PASTA**

**CHICKEN WITH CREAMY
MUSTARD SAUCE**

**CHICKEN WITH
MANGO SAUCE**

PASTA WITH CREAMY CHICKEN AND SPINACH

Remove skin from half a barbecued chicken. Shred meat. Cook 400 g (14 oz) penne pasta in pan of rapidly boiling water until just tender; drain. Heat 2 tablespoons oil in heavy-based frying pan. Add 2 onions, cut into wedges, and 2 crushed garlic cloves; stir over medium heat 3 minutes. Add 310 ml ($1^1/4$ cups) thick (double/heavy) cream and 60 ml ($1/4$ cup) chicken stock; simmer, uncovered, over low heat 2 minutes. Add 500 g (1 lb 2 oz) English spinach, trimmed, chicken and pasta. Stir over heat 1 minute or until heated through. Add salt and pepper. Serves 4.

CURRIED CHICKEN AND PASTA

Discard skin from a barbecued chicken. Shred meat. Cook 400 g (14 oz) spiral pasta in large pan of boiling water until tender; drain. Heat 2 tablespoons oil in large pan; add 1 chopped onion and $1^1/2$ tablespoons curry powder, stir over medium heat 1 minute. Add $1/2$ packet ($1^1/2$ cups) frozen mixed, diced vegetables, cook 3 minutes or until heated. Add 250 g (1 cup) sour cream, 1 tablespoon lemon juice and $1/2$ teaspoon pepper. Heat but do not boil. Add chicken and pasta, stir over heat until combined. Sprinkle with chopped parsley and chopped roasted cashew nuts. Serves 4.

CHICKEN WITH CREAMY MUSTARD SAUCE

Cut a small barbecued chicken into serving-sized pieces. Heat 2 tablespoons oil and fry 1 chopped onion until golden. Add 125 g ($4^1/2$ oz) sliced mushrooms, 80 ml ($1/3$ cup) white wine and simmer 1 minute. Lower heat and stir in 250 g (1 cup) sour cream, 2 tablespoons seeded mustard and $1/2$ teaspoon pepper, heat through but do not boil. Serve over chicken, garnished with 1 tablespoon chopped chives. Serves 4.

Fast-track FAVOURITE VEGETABLES

SWISS ONION TART

Preparation time: 15 minutes
Total cooking time: 55 minutes
Serves 4

2 sheets frozen shortcrust
    pastry, thawed
2 tablespoons oil
3 medium onions, sliced
125 g ($1/2$ cup) sour cream
2 eggs
65 g ($1/2$ cup) finely grated
    Gruyère cheese
cayenne pepper

➤ PREHEAT OVEN to 210°C (415°F/
Gas 6–7).
1 Fit pastry into a 20 cm (8 inch)
fluted flan tin; trim edges. Cut a sheet
of greaseproof paper large enough to
cover pastry-lined tin. Spread a layer
of dried beans or rice evenly over

paper. Bake for 10 minutes, remove
from oven. Discard paper and beans
or rice. Return pastry to oven for
5 minutes or until lightly golden.
Reduce oven to 180°C (350°F/Gas 4).
2 Heat oil in pan and add onion. Cook
over low heat, stirring often, for
15 minutes or until lightly browned
and very tender. Spread over pastry.
3 Whisk sour cream and eggs in bowl
until smooth; add cheese; stir until
combined. Place flan tin on baking
tray. Pour egg mixture over onion and
sprinkle lightly with cayenne. Bake
40 minutes or until filling is set. May be
garnished with fresh herbs.

COOK'S FILE

Storage time: Pastry can be cooked a
day in advance. Store, covered in plastic
wrap. Onion can be cooked and filling
prepared several hours ahead. Store,
covered, in refrigerator. Assemble tart
and bake just before serving.

MUSHROOM AND TOMATO TARTS

Preparation time: 10 minutes
Total cooking time: 22 minutes
Serves 4

1 sheet ready-rolled puff pastry
2 tablespoons soft cream
   cheese
2 tablespoons oil
100 g (3$^{1}/_{2}$ oz) button
   mushrooms, sliced
2 cloves garlic, crushed
$^{1}/_{2}$ teaspoon dried mixed herbs
4 cherry tomatoes, sliced
1 tablespoon grated Parmesan
   cheese

➤ PREHEAT OVEN to 240°C (475°F/
Gas 9). Brush an oven tray with
melted butter or oil.
1 Cut pastry into quarters. Place on
tray. Fold edges over to form a 1 cm
($^{1}/_{2}$ inch) border, press down firmly.
Spread cream cheese over pastry.
2 Heat oil in pan, add mushrooms,
garlic and herbs. Stir over medium
heat for 2 minutes or until softened
and lightly golden; drain on paper
towels. Arrange mushroom mixture
over cream cheese, top with tomato,
sprinkle with cheese. Bake 20 minutes
or until pastry is puffed and golden.

COOK'S FILE

Note: Drain vegetables well before
arranging over cream cheese.

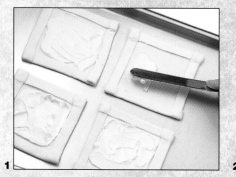

SALAD NIÇOISE

Preparation time: 10 minutes
Total cooking time: 10 minutes
Serves 4

16 baby potatoes
250 g (9 oz) green beans, sliced
    into short pieces
250 g (9 oz) cherry tomatoes,
    quartered
115 g (^{2}/3 cup) black olives
425 g (15 oz) can tuna, drained
    and flaked
100 g (3^1/2 oz) feta cheese, cubed
8 anchovies, chopped
80 ml (^{1}/3 cup) Italian dressing
4 hard-boiled eggs, quartered
1 lettuce, for serving

➤ COOK POTATOES in large pan of rapidly boiling water for 10 minutes or until tender; drain, cool.

1 Cook beans in medium pan of rapidly boiling water for 3 minutes or until tender; drain, cool. Cut potatoes into quarters.

2 Place potato quarters and beans in large bowl with tomato, olives, tuna, cheese, anchovies and dressing; stir until combined. Add eggs; stir gently to mix. Serve on a bed of lettuce.

COOK'S FILE

Storage time: Salad can be assembled several hours ahead. Store, covered, in refrigerator. Add dressing just before serving.

Note: Use home-made or commercial Italian dressing for this recipe.

CAESAR SALAD

Preparation time: 15 minutes
Total cooking time: 15 minutes
Serves 4

4 slices white bread
3 rashers bacon, chopped
1 cos (romaine) lettuce
50 g (1/2 cup) shaved Parmesan
  cheese

Dressing
4 anchovies, chopped
1 egg
1–2 tablespoons lemon juice
1 clove garlic, crushed
125 ml (1/2 cup) oil

➤ PREHEAT OVEN to 210°C (415°F/
Gas 6–7).

1 Remove crusts from bread, cut bread
into small cubes. Spread on a baking
tray and bake for 15 minutes or until
lightly golden. Fry bacon until crisp.
Drain on paper towels. Tear lettuce
leaves into bite-sized pieces. Combine in
a bowl with bread cubes, Parmesan and
bacon. Add Dressing, toss until combined, serve immediately.

2 To make Dressing: Place
anchovies, egg, lemon juice and garlic
in food processor or blender. Blend for
20 seconds or until smooth. With
motor constantly operating, add oil
slowly in a thin, steady stream,
processing until all oil is added and
dressing is thick and creamy.

COOK'S FILE

Storage time: Bread cubes can be
baked a day in advance. Store in an
airtight container. Dressing can also
be made a day in advance and
refrigerated in an airtight container.
Assemble salad just before serving.
Hint: Use a vegetable peeler to make
Parmesan cheese shavings.

CHEF'S SALAD

Preparation time: 15 minutes
Total cooking time: Nil
Serves 4

200 g (7 oz) mixed lettuce leaves
250 g (9 oz) leg ham, cut into
   strips
125 g (4$^1/_4$ oz) Swiss cheese
   slices, cut into strips
1 red capsicum (pepper), cut
   into strips
340 g (12 oz) can asparagus
   cuts, drained

Dressing
60 g ($^1/_4$ cup) mayonnaise
60 ml ($^1/_4$ cup) cream
1 tablespoon seeded mustard

➤ ARRANGE LETTUCE, ham, cheese, capsicum and asparagus on serving plates.

1 To make Dressing: Whisk the mayonnaise, cream and mustard for 1 minute or until combined. Drizzle Dressing over salad just before serving.

1

COOK'S FILE

Note: Mixed lettuce is available from greengrocers. However, any variety of lettuce is suitable for this salad.
Variation: Use blanched, fresh asparagus instead of canned asparagus, if preferred.

MIXED VEGETABLE CURRY

Preparation time: 10 minutes
Total cooking time: 25 minutes
Serves 4

1 tablespoon oil
1 onion, sliced
500 g (1 lb 2 oz) baby potatoes, quartered
250 g (9 oz) broccoli florets
2 large carrots, sliced
425 g (15 oz) can tomatoes
3 teaspoons curry paste
500 ml (2 cups) coconut milk
250 g (9 oz) small button mushrooms, halved

➤ HEAT OIL in a large pan and add sliced onion.

1 Stir over medium heat for 3–5 minutes or until golden. Add potato, broccoli, carrot, undrained, crushed tomato and curry paste; stir to combine. Add coconut milk to pan; bring to the boil. Reduce heat to low, simmer, uncovered, for 15 minutes or until vegetables are almost tender.

2 Add mushrooms and cook for another 5 minutes or until vegetables are tender.

COOK'S FILE

Storage time: This dish can be made a day in advance. Store, covered, in refrigerator. Reheat gently just before serving.

CAULIFLOWER WITH TOMATO SAUCE

Preparation time: 20 minutes
Total cooking time: 20–25 minutes
Serves 4

800 g (1 lb 12 oz) cauliflower
2–3 tablespoons olive oil
80 g (1 cup) coarse fresh white
  breadcrumbs
500 g (2 cups) bottled tomato
  pasta sauce
2 tablespoons shredded basil
  leaves
50 g ($^1/_2$ cup) grated Parmesan
  cheese
60 g ($^1/_2$ cup) grated Cheddar
  cheese

➤ TRIM cauliflower into small florets.
1 Preheat oven to 180°C (350°F/ Gas 4). Brush a deep ovenproof dish with melted butter or oil. Place florets in dish. Heat oil in a frying pan; add the fresh breadcrumbs and toss over medium heat until crisp and golden. Season with salt and pepper. Remove from pan and drain on paper towels.
2 Combine tomato pasta sauce and basil. Pour over cauliflower in prepared dish. Sprinkle with combined breadcrumbs and cheeses. Sprinkle with extra pepper. Bake for 20–25 minutes or until cauliflower is tender, cheese has melted and top is brown.

COOK'S FILE

Note: Choose a chunky tomato pasta sauce for this dish.

87

LEEK AND ASPARAGUS FRITTATA

Preparation time: 10 minutes
Total cooking time: 35 minutes
Serves 4

30 g (1 oz) butter
1 leek, finely sliced
340 g (12 oz) can asparagus
   cuts, drained
2 tablespoons chopped
   sundried tomatoes
5 eggs
125 ml (¹/₂ cup)
   cream

➤ PREHEAT OVEN to 180°C
(350°F/Gas 4). Grease a 23 cm (9 inch)
pie plate or flan dish.
1 Melt butter in pan and add sliced
leek. Stir over medium heat for
2 minutes or until softened. Drain on
paper towels.
2 Combine leek, asparagus and sundried tomatoes in a bowl. Spread
evenly into prepared dish. Whisk
eggs, cream, salt and pepper together
and pour over vegetables. Bake for
30 minutes or until golden brown.

COOK'S FILE

Note: Sundried tomatoes are available
from supermarkets and delicatessens.

GRILLED VEGETABLES WITH ROSEMARY AND GARLIC

Preparation time: 10 minutes
Total cooking time: 15 minutes
Serves 4

2 large orange sweet potatoes
2 large red capsicums (peppers)
6 medium zucchini (courgettes), sliced in half lengthways
4 large mushroom caps

Dressing
80 ml (¹/₃ cup) olive oil
2 tablespoons balsamic vinegar
2 tablespoons chopped rosemary
3 cloves garlic, crushed

➤ CUT SWEET POTATOES into thick slices.

1 Remove seeds and membrane from capsicum. Cut flesh in thick strips. Place with zucchini and mushroom caps on a cold, lightly oiled griller (broiler) tray, brush with Dressing. Cook under high heat for 15 minutes or until vegetables are tender and lightly golden, turning occasionally. Brush with remaining Dressing several times during cooking.

2 To make Dressing: Place oil, vinegar, rosemary, garlic, salt and pepper in a bowl; whisk to combine.

COOK'S FILE

Storage time: Cook vegetables just before serving. Dressing can be prepared and stored in refrigerator.

1

2

CORN AND CAPSICUM FRITTERS

Preparation time: 20 minutes
Total cooking time: 10 minutes
Serves 4

1 large red capsicum (pepper)
2–3 cobs 300 g (10½ oz) fresh
    corn kernels
oil, for frying
2 tablespoons chopped parsley,
    coriander (cilantro) leaves,
    chives or dill
3 eggs

➤ CUT CAPSICUM into large pieces and chop into small dice.

1 Scrape kernels from the fresh corn, using a sharp knife.

2 Heat 2 tablespoons of the oil in a large frying pan. Add the corn kernels and stir over medium heat for 2 minutes. Add the red capsicum, stir for another 2 minutes. Transfer vegetables to a medium bowl. Add herbs and stir well to combine. Beat eggs in a small jug with pepper and salt, to taste. Stir egg gradually into the vegetable mixture.

3 Heat a non-stick frying pan over medium heat. Add oil to cover base.

Drop large spoonfuls of the vegetable mixture at a time into oil. Cook 1–2 minutes or until brown. Turn; cook other side. Drain on paper towels; keep warm. Serve garnished with a parsley sprig, if desired.

COOK'S FILE

Hint: The fritters may be served with sour cream and a crisp green salad for lunch or as accompaniment to a main course.

Note: These fritters contain no flour, so they cook quickly. They should still be a little creamy in the middle when served.

ONION AND PARMESAN PILAF

Preparation time: 5 minutes
Total cooking time: 20 minutes
Serves 6

60 g (2¼ oz) butter
3 onions, sliced
2 cloves garlic, crushed
2 cups (200 g) basmati rice
1.25 litres (5 cups) vegetable
   stock
235 g (1½ cups) shelled
   peas
50 g (½ cup) grated Parmesan
   cheese
30 g (½ cup) chopped parsley

➤ MELT BUTTER in large pan, add onion and garlic and stir over low heat for 5 minutes or until soft and golden.

1 Add rice and stock, bring to the boil; stir once. Reduce heat to low, simmer for 5 minutes or until almost all the liquid has been absorbed.

2 Add peas, stir until combined. Cover pan, cook over very low heat for another 10 minutes or until rice is tender. Stir in Parmesan cheese and parsley and serve immediately.

COOK'S FILE

Hint: Serve as a side dish with a barbecued chicken.
Note: Basmati rice is a fragrant rice available from supermarkets and delicatessens.

HERBED POTATO PANCAKES

Preparation time: 10 minutes
Total cooking time: 12 minutes
Makes 10–12 pancakes

2 tablespoons chopped chives
2 tablespoons chopped tarragon
  or parsley
600 g (1 lb 5 oz) potatoes,
  peeled
60 g (2¼ oz) unsalted
  butter
2 tablespoons olive oil

➤ MIX CHIVES, tarragon or parsley and salt and pepper in a bowl.

1 Coarsely grate the potatoes into a large bowl. Add herb mixture and stir to combine.

2 Heat half the butter and oil in large non-stick frying pan, over medium heat, until starting to foam. Cook heaped tablespoonsful of mixture for 2 minutes. Turn and cook for approximately 2–3 minutes or until golden. Drain on paper towels; keep warm. Add remaining butter and oil to pan. Repeat process until all mixture is used.

COOK'S FILE

Storage time: Pancakes may be kept for up to ½ hour, loosely covered with foil, in a 120°C (250°F/Gas ½) oven.

Note: Work quickly when grating potato. Potato can be grated using a food processor if preferred. Cook mixture immediately after it has been prepared to prevent the potato from discolouring. A starchy liquid will form in the bowl. Don't discard, mix into the pancakes.

Variations: Substitute parsnip or carrot for one of the potatoes.

Substitute chopped dill for the tarragon or parsley.

EGGPLANT SANDWICHES

Preparation time: 10 minutes +
  30 minutes standing
Total cooking time: 20 minutes
Serves 4

3 medium eggplant
  (aubergines)
olive oil, for frying
ground cumin, optional
2 red capsicums (peppers)
10–12 sundried tomatoes
200 g (7 oz) ricotta or goats
  cheese
20 g (¹/₃ cup) shredded basil
  leaves
basil leaves, extra

➤ SLICE EGGPLANT lengthways,
about 1 cm (¹/₂ inch) thick.
1 Choose the 8 largest slices and lay
on a tray or board. Reserve the rest.
(see Note). Sprinkle eggplant with salt.
Allow to stand for 30 minutes. Rinse
well and pat dry with paper towels.
2 Heat a large frying pan over
medium heat. Add oil to cover base of
pan. When hot add eggplant slices, a
few at a time. Cook for 2–3 minutes
each side or until brown. Drain on
paper towels. Season each slice with
salt and pepper. Sprinkle with cumin,
if desired.
3 Cut capsicum into large pieces.
Remove seeds and membrane. Place
cut-side down on cold griller (broiler)
tray. Brush skin with oil. Cook under
preheated griller (broiler) until skin
blackens and blisters. Cover with
damp tea-towel until cool. Peel off
skin and cut into strips.
4 Cut the sundried tomatoes into
strips. On each of 4 serving plates,
place a slice of eggplant. Spread slices
with ricotta or goats cheese. Top with
sundried tomato and capsicum,
reserving some for garnish. Sprinkle
with basil. Cover each with a second
slice of eggplant. Decorate top with
crossed strips of capsicum and sundried
tomato. Garnish with extra basil leaves.

C O O K ' S   F I L E

Note: Unused eggplant will last a day
or two in the refrigerator. Finely chop
and brown in olive oil with crushed
garlic, season well. Spread on toast for
a snack or add to a soup or casserole.

WARM BEAN SALAD

Preparation time: 10 minutes
Total cooking time: 8 minutes
Serves 4

2 tablespoons olive oil
1 medium onion, finely chopped
1 clove garlic, crushed
1 small red capsicum (pepper),
  cut into short strips
75 g (2 1/2 oz) green beans, cut
  into 2 cm (3/4 inch) lengths
50 g (1 3/4 oz) button
  mushrooms, sliced
1 tablespoon balsamic vinegar
430 g (15 oz) can three-bean mix

➤ HEAT HALF the oil in a pan.
1 Add onion and cook for 2 minutes over medium heat. Add garlic, capsicum, green beans, mushrooms and vinegar. Cook for another 5 minutes, stirring occasionally. Thoroughly rinse and drain bean mix. Add to vegetables with remaining oil, stir until just warmed through.

1

COOK'S FILE

Storage time: May be kept for 1 day in refrigerator. Reheat for serving.
Hint: This salad is delicious as an accompaniment to roast lamb. Serve with toasted thick Italian bread for a vegetarian main meal.

TWO-POTATO GRATIN

Preparation time: 15 minutes
Total cooking time: 45 minutes
Serves 4

4 small potatoes
1 large orange sweet potato
1 small onion, thinly sliced
125 ml ($^1/_2$ cup) chicken stock
65 g ($^1/_2$ cup) finely grated
   Gruyère cheese

➤ PREHEAT OVEN to 180°C (350°F/ Gas 4). Grease a shallow 2-litre (4 cup) ovenproof dish.

1 Peel potatoes and sweet potato and cut into slices. Place potato and onion in prepared dish in alternating layers. Pour chicken stock over potato, sprinkle evenly with cheese and bake for 45 minutes, or until golden brown.

1

COOK'S FILE

Variation: Cheddar cheese may be used instead of Gruyère.

No-effort DELICIOUS DESSERTS

BANANA FRITTERS WITH CARAMEL SAUCE

Preparation time: 10 minutes
Total cooking time: 10 minutes
Serves 4

125 g (1 cup) self-raising flour
1 egg, beaten
185 ml (³/4 cup) soda water
oil, for deep-frying
4 bananas, each cut into
    quarters
ice-cream, for serving

Caramel Sauce
185 g (1 cup) soft brown sugar
125 ml (¹/2 cup) cream
100 g (3¹/2 oz) butter, chopped

➤ SIFT FLOUR into medium bowl; make a well in the centre.
1 Add egg and soda water all at once. Stir until all liquid is incorporated and batter is free of lumps.
2 Heat oil in heavy-based pan. Dip bananas in batter a few pieces at a time; drain off excess batter. Gently lower bananas into moderately hot oil. Cook over medium–high heat for 2 minutes or until golden, crisp and warmed through. Carefully remove from oil with a slotted spoon. Drain on paper towels; keep warm. Repeat with remaining bananas. Serve fritters immediately with ice-cream and caramel sauce.
3 To make Caramel Sauce: Combine all ingredients in a small pan and stir until sugar has dissolved and butter has melted. Bring to the boil; reduce heat and simmer for 2 minutes.

COOK'S FILE

Storage time: Bananas fritters are best cooked just before serving.
Hint: To prevent discolouration of bananas, don't cut them until you are ready to use them.
Variations: Serve banana fritters with chocolate, strawberry or mocha sauce or drizzle with honey.
  If you prefer, fritters can be served without sauce. Simply sprinkle with sifted icing (confectioners) sugar and serve with cream or vanilla ice-cream.

PEARS IN RED WINE

Preparation time: 20 minutes
Total cooking time: 55 minutes
Serves 4

4 firm pears
750 ml (3 cups) good-quality
   red wine
185 g ($^3/_4$ cup) caster
   (superfine) sugar
1 cinnamon stick
60 ml ($^1/_4$ cup) orange juice
5 cm (2 inch) piece orange
   zest
200 g (7 oz) mascarpone cheese

➤ PEEL PEARS, being careful to keep them whole with stalks attached.
1 Place wine, sugar, cinnamon stick, orange juice and zest in a large pan. Stir over heat until sugar is dissolved; add cinnamon and rind. Add pears, stir gently to coat. Cover pan; simmer for 20–25 minutes or until pears are cooked. Allow to cool in syrup.
2 Remove pears and drain on paper towels. Bring liquid to boil and boil rapidly without lid until only 185 ml ($^3/_4$ cup) liquid remains. Serve pears with a little syrup and mascarpone.

COOK'S FILE

Storage time: Pears may be cooked several hours ahead.
Hint: Pan must be of suitable size to hold pears upright. The pears should be almost covered with wine mixture.

1

2

FRUIT MEDLEY BREAD PUDDING

Preparation time: 15 minutes
Total cooking time: 1 hour
Serves 4

5 slices white bread
30 g (1 oz) butter
140 g ($^{3}/_{4}$ cup) dried fruit medley
4 eggs
625 ml ($2^{1}/_{2}$ cups) milk
90 g ($^{1}/_{3}$ cup) caster (superfine) sugar
$^{1}/_{2}$ teaspoon ground cinnamon

➤ PREHEAT OVEN to 160°C (315°F/ Gas 2–3).
1 Remove crusts from bread and spread bread with butter. Cut slices diagonally in half. Place half the bread, buttered-side up, in a 1.5-litre (6 cup) ovenproof dish. Top with the fruit medley and remaining bread, buttered-side up.
2 Whisk eggs, milk and sugar in a large jug until combined. Pour over bread. Sprinkle with cinnamon. Place dish in a shallow baking dish. Pour in enough hot water to come halfway up the sides. Bake 1 hour or until set and lightly golden. Remove dish from water immediately.

COOK'S FILE

Storage time: Serve warm or at room temperature. If serving at room temperature, cook several hours ahead.

APRICOT AND MACADAMIA NUT ICE-CREAM

Preparation time: 10 minutes
Total cooking time: Nil
Serves 4

2 cups (500 ml) vanilla ice-cream, softened slightly
70 g (½ cup) chopped, roasted, unsalted macadamia nuts
30 g (¼ cup) chopped plain, sweet biscuits
60 g (¼ cup) chopped glacé apricots

➤ PLACE ALL ingredients in a medium bowl.
1 Stir until combined. Spoon mixture into 4 serving glasses, freeze until firm.

COOK'S FILE

Storage time: This recipe can be made a day ahead. Store in freezer.
Variation: Add 2 tablespoons of Grand Marnier.

CITRUS DELICIOUS

Preparation time: 15 minutes
Total cooking time: 1 hour
Serves 4

60 g (½ cup) self-raising flour
250 g (1 cup) caster (superfine)
    sugar
2 teaspoons grated orange
    zest
80 ml (⅓ cup) orange juice
125 ml (½ cup) lemon juice
125 g (4½ oz) butter, melted
250 ml (1 cup) milk
3 eggs, separated

➤ PREHEAT OVEN to 180°C (350°F/ Gas 4). Lightly grease a 1.5-litre (6 cup) ovenproof dish.

1 Sift flour into a large bowl. Add sugar, stir until combined. Combine orange zest, orange juice, lemon juice, butter, milk and egg yolks in a bowl; whisk lightly until smooth. Add to flour mixture, stir until combined.

2 Beat egg whites in small mixing bowl with electric beaters until stiff peaks form. Using metal spoon, fold gently into mixture. Pour mixture into prepared dish.

3 Place dish in a shallow baking dish. Pour enough hot water in baking dish to come halfway up the side. Bake for 1 hour or until firm in the centre. Remove dish from water immediately.

COOK'S FILE

Storage time: Best eaten on day of baking. Serve warm or at room temperature.

Hint: If Citrus Delicious becomes too brown on the top before the centre is firm, cover dish with foil.

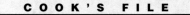

DREAMY *Desserts* IN MINUTES

BERRIES WITH BERRY SWIRL CREAM

Combine 250 g (9 oz) halved strawberries with 100 g ($3^1/2$ oz) raspberries, pulp of 2 passionfruit and 2 tablespoons sugar. Spoon into serving dishes. Using electric beaters, beat 125 ml ($^1/2$ cup) cream in small bowl until soft peaks form. Place an extra 100 g ($3^1/2$ oz) raspberries in small bowl; mash lightly with a fork. Add to cream and stir until raspberries form swirls in the cream; spoon over strawberry mixture. Serves 4.

CHOCOLATE MINT MOUSSE

Place 200 g (7 oz) chopped, dark chocolate in small heat-proof bowl. Stand bowl over pan of simmering water; stir until chocolate has melted and mixture is smooth, cool slightly. Using electric beaters, beat 310 ml ($1^1/4$ cups) thick (double/heavy) cream until stiff peaks form. Add melted chocolate to cream with 8 chopped after-dinner mints and stir until combined. Spoon into 4 serving glasses, refrigerate for 1 hour or until firm. Decorate with extra after-dinner mints, if desired. Serves 4.

COFFEE CREAM WHIP

Using electric beaters, beat 2 eggs and 2 tablespoons caster (superfine) sugar for 3 minutes or until thick and pale. Dissolve 1 tablespoon of instant coffee powder in 2 teaspoons hot water and add to mixture with 250 ml (1 cup) thick (double/heavy) cream. Beat for 3 minutes or until soft peaks form. Add 8 roughly chopped sponge finger biscuits and 2 tablespoons brandy; stir until combined. Spoon into serving dishes. Refrigerate for at least 1 hour; serve dusted with cocoa. Serves 4.

BERRIES WITH BERRY SWIRL CREAM

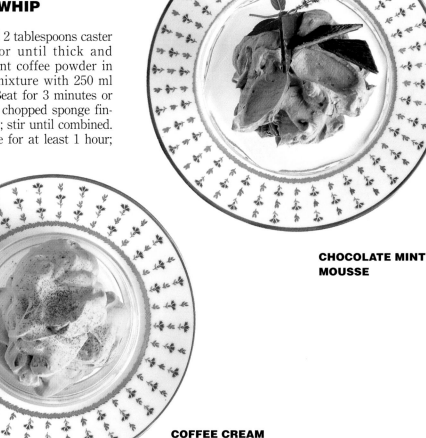

CHOCOLATE MINT MOUSSE

COFFEE CREAM WHIP

AND MARNIER
TRAWBERRIES

POACHED APPLES WITH ORANGE
SEGMENTS AND CHOCOLATE SAUCE

GINGER COCONUT
PEACHES

BUTTERY POACHED
FRUITS

GRAND MARNIER STRAWBERRIES

Combine 125 g ($1/2$ cup) sugar, 250 ml (1 cup) water and 2 tablespoons lemon juice in a pan; stir over medium heat until sugar is dissolved; bring to the boil. Reduce heat to low and simmer, uncovered, for 5 minutes or until mixture becomes slightly syrupy. Remove from heat, stir in 60 ml ($1/4$ cup) Grand Marnier and 500 g (1 lb 2 oz) halved strawberries. Serve warm or cool with ice-cream or cream. Serves 4.

POACHED APPLES WITH ORANGE SEGMENTS AND CHOCOLATE SAUCE

Combine 170 ml ($2/3$ cup) water and 125 g ($1/2$ cup) sugar in a large pan and stir over heat until the sugar is dissolved. Add 3 Granny Smith apples, peeled and cut into wedges; bring to the boil. Reduce heat to low and cover pan. Simmer, stirring occasionally, for 2 minutes or until apples are tender; allow to cool. Add 3 oranges, segmented, and 2 teaspoons grated orange zest. Combine 125 ml ($1/2$ cup) thick (double/heavy) cream in medium pan with 125 g ($4 1/2$ oz) chopped dark chocolate and 60 g ($2 1/4$ oz) butter. Stir over low heat for 1 minute or until chocolate has melted and mixture is smooth. Spoon apples and oranges into serving dishes with a little of the cooking liquid. Top with chocolate sauce. Decorate with some chocolate pieces, if desired. Serves 4.

GINGER COCONUT PEACHES

Preheat oven to 210°C (415°F/Gas 6–7). Drain an 825 g (1 lb 13 oz) can peach halves and place, cut-side up, on a tray. Combine 45 g ($1/2$ cup) desiccated coconut, 45 g ($1/4$ cup) soft brown sugar, 8 crushed ginger biscuits, 2 teaspoons grated lemon zest, 1 teaspoon mixed spice and 60 g ($2 1/4$ oz) softened butter. Spoon mixture onto peach halves. Bake for 10 minutes or until the topping is golden brown. Serve with cream or ice-cream, decorated with strips of lemon zest, if desired. Serves 4.

BUTTERY POACHED FRUITS

Combine 300 g ($10 1/2$ oz) dried fruit salad (whole dried fruits) in a medium pan with 50 g ($1 3/4$ oz) butter, 125 ml ($1/2$ cup) orange juice, 2 tablespoons rum, 1 teaspoon mixed spice and 45 g ($1/4$ cup) soft brown sugar. Bring to the boil and simmer, covered, for 12 minutes or until the fruit has softened. Serve warm with ice-cream. Garnish with some thin strips of orange zest, if desired. Serves 4.

BAKED CUSTARD

Preparation time: 5 minutes
Total cooking time: 35 minutes
Serves 4

3 eggs
95 g ($^1/_2$ cup) soft brown sugar
375 ml (1$^1/_2$ cups) milk
125 ml ($^1/_2$ cup) cream
1 teaspoon vanilla essence
ground nutmeg, for dusting

➤ PREHEAT OVEN to 180°C (350°F/ Gas 4). Brush a 1-litre (4 cup) capacity ovenproof dish with melted butter.

1 Whisk eggs, sugar, milk, cream and vanilla in medium bowl for 1 minute. Pour into prepared dish.

2 Place filled dish into a shallow baking dish. Pour enough hot water into baking dish to come halfway up the sides. Place on oven shelf, sprinkle top of custard with nutmeg; bake for 15 minutes. Reduce heat to 160°C (315°F/Gas 2–3), bake for another 20 minutes or until custard is set and a sharp knife comes out clean when inserted. Remove dish from water immediately. Serve warm or cold.

COOK'S FILE

Storage time: Mixture can be prepared several hours ahead. If serving warm, cook just before serving. If serving cold, custard can be cooked a day in advance. Store, covered, in refrigerator.
Hint: Serve custard on its own or with fresh, poached or canned fruit.

APPLE PUFF SQUARES

Preparation time: 15 minutes
Total cooking time: 15 minutes
Serves 4

1 sheet ready-rolled puff pastry
60 g (2¼ oz) butter, melted
2 tablespoons soft brown sugar
½ teaspoon ground mixed spice
2 medium Granny Smith apples

➤ PREHEAT OVEN to 210°C (415°F/
Gas 6–7). Cut pastry into 4 squares,
place on an oven tray. Combine butter,
sugar and spice, brush half the mixture
over pastry squares.
1 Peel apples, cut into wedges,
remove core. Cut apple into very thin
slices, lay on top of pastry squares
leaving a 1 cm (½ inch) border.
2 Brush squares with remaining
butter mixture. Bake for 15 minutes or
until apple is tender and lightly
golden. Cut each in half for serving.

COOK'S FILE

Storage time: Cook this dish just
before serving.

SELF-SAUCING BAKED CHOCOLATE PUDDING

Preparation time: 25 minutes
Total cooking time: 40 minutes
Serves 4–6

125 g (1 cup) self-raising flour
2 tablespoons cocoa powder
125 g (½ cup) caster (superfine) sugar
125 ml (½ cup) milk

1 egg
60 g (2¼ oz) butter, melted
1 teaspoon vanilla essence
2 tablespoons cocoa powder, extra
185 g (¾ cup) caster (superfine) sugar, extra

➤ PREHEAT OVEN to 180°C (350°F/ Gas 4). Brush a 2-litre (8 cup) oven-proof dish with melted butter or oil.
1 Sift dry ingredients into a large mixing bowl; make a well in the centre.
2 Pour in combined milk, egg, butter and essence. Stir until smooth; do not over-beat. Pour into prepared dish. Dissolve extra cocoa powder and sugar in 625 ml (2½ cups) boiling water. Pour gently over the back of a spoon onto the pudding mixture.
3 Bake for 40 minutes or until a skewer comes out clean when inserted. Top may be dusted with sifted icing (confectioners) sugar.

COOK'S FILE

Hint: Serve with some of the sauce.

ORANGE BANANA CREPES

Preparation time: 15 minutes
Total cooking time: 15 minutes
Serves 4

85 g ($^2/_3$ cup) self-raising flour
2 eggs
125 ml ($^1/_2$ cup) milk
60 g ($2^1/_4$ oz) butter
60 g ($^1/_3$ cup) soft brown sugar
3 teaspoons grated orange zest
60 ml ($^1/_4$ cup) orange juice
3 bananas, sliced

➤ SIFT FLOUR into a medium bowl; make a well in the centre.

1 Whisk eggs, milk and 60 ml ($^1/_4$ cup) water until combined. Add gradually to flour. Stir until the liquid is incorporated and batter is free of lumps. Pour 2–3 tablespoons of batter onto lightly greased 20 cm (8 inch) non-stick pan; swirl evenly over base.

Cook over medium heat for 1 minute or until underside is golden. Turn crepe over; cook other side. Transfer to a plate; cover with a tea-towel, keep warm. Repeat process with remaining batter, greasing pan when necessary. You will need 8 crepes for this recipe.

2 Heat butter in medium pan, add sugar and stir over low heat until sugar is dissolved and mixture is bubbling. Add zest and juice. Bring to boil; reduce heat. Simmer, uncovered, for 2 minutes. Add banana; simmer for 1 minute. Divide mixture among the 8 crepes. Fold crepes into quarters to enclose. Place crepes on serving plates.

COOK'S FILE

Storage time: Batter can be made several hours in advance. Leave, covered with plastic wrap. Cook crepes just before serving. Alternatively, crepes can be cooked several hours in advance. Place on a baking tray; cover with aluminium foil. Just before serving, place crepes in 180°C (350°F/ Gas 4) oven for 10 minutes or until warmed through.

PEACHES AND CREAM TRIFLE

Preparation time: 20 minutes
Total cooking time: Nil
Serves 6–8

825 g (1 lb 13 oz) can sliced
    peaches
60 ml ($^1/4$ cup) marsala
1 day-old sponge cake, cut into
    cubes
250 ml (1 cup) cream
220 g (1 cup) mascarpone
25 g ($^1/4$ cup) flaked almonds,
    toasted

➤ DRAIN PEACHES, reserving 125 ml ($^1/2$ cup) juice.

1 Combine marsala and reserved juice. Place sponge cake cubes in a 2-litre (8 cup) dish and press down firmly. Drizzle with marsala mixture.

2 Arrange peaches over cake. Using electric beaters, beat cream until soft peaks form. Add mascarpone and beat until just combined. Spread mixture over peaches. Refrigerate for 1 hour to allow flavours to develop. Sprinkle with almonds just before serving.

COOK'S FILE

Variation: Replace marsala with peach schnapps or Grand Marnier.

APPLE BETTY

Preparation time: 15 minutes
Total cooking time: 25 minutes
Serves 6

2 x 410 g (14 oz) cans pie apple
5 slices fruit bread
40 g (1¹/₂ oz) soft butter
2 teaspoons cinnamon sugar

➤ PREHEAT OVEN to 180°C (350°F/ Gas 4).

1 Spread apple over base of 1.5-litre (6 cup) ovenproof dish. Cut crusts from bread, spread both sides with butter. Sprinkle 1 side with cinnamon sugar. Cut into cubes and arrange bread in an even layer over apple. Bake for 25 minutes or until golden.

QUICK PAVLOVAS

Preparation time: 15 minutes
Total cooking time: Nil
Serves 6

300 g (10^1/$_4$ oz) packet frozen
  raspberries
310 ml (1^1/$_4$ cups) cream
18 small meringues
2 flaky chocolate bars, roughly
  broken

➤ THAW RASPBERRIES according
to directions on the packet.
1 Using electric beaters, whip cream
until soft peaks form. Fold raspberries
through cream until just combined.

Arrange meringues on serving plates.
Spread cream mixture over and sprinkle with chocolate shards.

1

Variation: Use chopped, fresh strawberries or drained canned fruit.

INDEX

USEFUL INFORMATION

All our recipes are tested in a special test kitchen. Standard metric measuring cups and spoons are used in the development of our recipes. All cup and spoon measurements are level. We have used 60 g (2¼ oz/Grade 3) eggs in all recipes. Sizes of cans vary from manufacturer to manufacturer and between countries—use the can size closest to the one suggested in the recipe.

Conversion Guide

1 cup	= 250 ml (9 fl oz)
1 teaspoon	= 5 ml
1 Australian tablespoon	= 20 ml (4 teaspoons)
1 UK/US tablespoon	= 15 ml (3 teaspoons)

NOTE: We have used 20 ml tablespoon measures. If you are using a 15 ml tablespoon, for most recipes the difference will not be noticeable. However, for recipes using baking powder, gelatine, bicarbonate of soda, small amounts of flour and cornflour, add an extra teaspoon for each tablespoon specified.

Dry Measures

30 g	= 1 oz
250 g	= 9 oz
500 g	= 1 lb 2 oz

Liquid Measures

30 ml	= 1 fl oz
125 ml	= 4½ fl oz
250 ml	= 9 fl oz

Linear Measures

6 mm	= ¼ inch
1 cm	= ½ inch
2.5 cm	= 1 inch

Cup Conversions

1 cup flour, plain (all-purpose) or self-raising	= 125 g (4½ oz)
1 cup wholemeal flour	= 150 g (5½ oz)
1 cup desiccated coconut	= 90 g (3¼ oz)
1 cup sultanas	= 125 g (4½ oz)
1 cup polenta (cornmeal)	= 150 g (5½ oz)
1 cup granulated sugar	= 250 g (9 oz)
1 cup icing (confectioners') sugar	= 125 g (4½ oz)

Oven Temperatures

Cooking times may vary slightly depending on the type of oven you are using. Before you preheat the oven, we suggest that you refer to the manufacturer's instructions to ensure proper temperature control.

	°C	°F	Gas Mark
Very slow	120	250	½
Slow	150	300	2
Warm	170	325	3
Moderate	180	350	4
Mod. hot	190	375	5
Mod. hot	200	400	6
Hot	220	425	7
Very hot	230	450	8

NOTE: For fan-forced ovens check your appliance manual, but as a general rule, set oven temperature to 20°C lower than the temperature indicated in the recipe.

International Glossary

bicarbonate of soda	baking soda
chilli	chili pepper, chile
golden syrup	use dark corn syrup
soft brown sugar	light brown sugar
silverbeet	Swiss chard
sweet potato	kumera

This edition published in 2003 by Bay Books, an imprint of Murdoch Magazines Pty Limited, GPO Box 1203, Sydney NSW 2001, Australia.

Editorial Director: Diana Hill. **Editor:** Wendy Stephen.
Food Director: Lulu Grimes.
Food Editors: Kerrie Ray, Tracy Rutherford.
Creative Director: Marylouise Brammer.
Designer: Lena Lowe.
Assistant Designer: Michele Lichtenberger.
Recipe Development: Wendy Berecry, Janelle Bloom, Michelle Earl, Rachel Mackey, Rosemary Penman.
Food Stylist: Mary Harris.
Photographers: Luis Martin, Reg Morrison (Steps).
Food Preparation: Christine Sheppard.

Chief Executive: Juliet Rogers. **Publisher:** Kay Scarlett.

ISBN 0 86411 443 5.
Reprinted 2004. Printed by Sing Cheong Printing Co. Ltd. PRINTED IN CHINA.

1 cm
2 cm
3 cm
4 cm
5 cm
6 cm
7 cm
8 cm
9 cm
10 cm
11 cm
12 cm
13 cm
14 cm
15 cm
16 cm
17 cm
18 cm
19 cm
20 cm
21 cm
22 cm
23 cm
24 cm
25 cm